For Ray and Robert Hussa

MAINTAINING OUR DIFFERENCES

Maintaining our Differences
Minority families in multicultural societies

Edited by

CAROL D.H. HARVEY
University of Manitoba, Canada

Ashgate

Aldershot • Burlington USA • Singapore • Sydney

Published by
Ashgate Publishing Limited
Gower House
Croft Road
Aldershot
Hampshire GU11 3HR
England

Ashgate Publishing Company
131 Main Street
Burlington, VT 05401-5600 USA

Ashgate website: http://www.ashgate.com

British Library Cataloguing in Publication Data
Maintaining our differences : minority families in
    multicultural societies. - (Interdisciplinary research
    series in ethnic, gender and class relations)
    1. Minorities 2. Pluralism (Social sciences) 3. Family
    I. Harvey, Carol D.H.
    305.8

Library of Congress Control Number: 2001087938

ISBN 0 7546 1246 5

Printed and bound by Athenaeum Press, Ltd.,
Gateshead, Tyne & Wear.

Contents

List of Tables

List of Figures

List of Contributors

Carol D. H. Harvey, Ph.D., is Professor, Department of Family Studies, Faculty of Human Ecology, University of Manitoba, Winnipeg, Canada. She is interested in family interaction, especially within minority groups.

Fatima Husain, Ph.D., worked as a Research Fellow at the University of North London, on a European Union project on Muslim Families. She is currently working as an independent research consultant.

Rachel Lawrenchuk is a Ph.D. student in the Department of Community Health Sciences, Faculty of Medicine, University of Manitoba. Her research interest is Aboriginal child and family education.

Margaret O'Brien, formerly at the University of North London, is now with the School of Social Work and Psychosocial Studies at the University of East Anglia.

John E. Peters, Ph.D., is Professor, Department of Sociology and Anthropology, Development and International Studies, Wilfrid Laurier University, Waterloo, Ontario, Canada. In addition to studying Mennonites, he spent eight years in the Amazon of Brazil studying the Yanomani peoples.

Darren E. Sherkat, Ph.D., is Associate Professor, Sociology and Religious Studies, Vanderbilt University, Nashville, Tennessee, U.S.A. Much of his work examines religious change in the United States, with a particular emphasis on fundamentalism and African American religion.

Susan C. Ziehl, Ph.D., is Senior Lecturer, Department of Sociology and Industrial Sociology, Rhodes University, Grahamstown, South Africa. She studies the much-neglected question of culture and its impact on household formation.

Acknowledgements

The audiences at the Committee on Family Research (RC-06), of the International Sociological Association's XIV Congress in Montreal, held in July 1998, were treated to a series of papers by authors who have written Chapters 1-4 of this book. The mechanisms by which minority families interact with the dominant cultures in which they live can now reach a wider audience.

Thank you to the authors of the chapters presented here. Your scholarship shows insight into minority and majority cultures. You were patient, helpful and co-operative.

The help of the University of Manitoba in providing time, space and equipment is appreciated. Securing the publisher was done while on sabbatical as a Research Associate, International Social Science Institute, University of Edinburgh, and I was generously given space and equipment while I was there.

Production assistance was given by Pauline Chambers, Ile-des-Chênes, Manitoba. Having a competent technical assistant is crucial; Pauline's cheerful wit is a bonus.

Ashgate Publishing reaches many readers with its support of the social sciences and humanities. Special thanks to Sarah Markham, Anne Kierby, and others at Ashgate. You have been very helpful and professional.

Finally, my own family have provided inspiration and encouragement. My father, the late Arthur Hussa and my mother Ruth Hussa, showed me appreciation of people in many walks of life. My husband Mahlon understands the value of cultural diversity, and he was willing to commit help and money to see this book in print. Our daughters, son-in law, and granddaughter give joy and affection. I am indebted to all of you.

C. D. H. Harvey, Editor

Introduction

CAROL D.H. HARVEY

Families who are part of a minority group within a dominant culture use various ways of maintaining their differences. In this collection researchers explore minority families in four countries. These families use the values of their religion to help define them and keep their subcultures alive. They are also influenced by the dominant cultures around them. Some of these minority families use distinctive dress or language, which also reinforce their separation from the dominant culture.

In the four countries where the research took place, Canada, the United States, the United Kingdom, and South Africa, are all multicultural. Although the social situations differ in these countries, they are all industrialised, and to varying degrees, are democracies whose people hold post-modern values. The dominant language spoken is English, and, although sometimes in a statistical minority, the power brokers are white. The five minority cultures all begin life with another language and are introduced to English later, generally in school.

Old Order Mennonites in Canada were studied by John Peters, Pakistanis in Great Britain by Fatima Husain and Margaret O'Brien, conservative Christians in the United States by Darren Sherkat, Afrikaaners and whites in South Africa by Susan Ziehl, and Cree and Ojibway in Canada by Rachel Lawrenchuk and myself.

First, John Peters of Wilfred Laurier University in Canada uses an ethnographic, developmental approach to study Old Order Mennonites. These conservative Christian families are farmers and pacifists. Value is placed on a peaceful, rural way of living. Parents try to find money to establish their adult sons in farming. Roles of men and women are prescribed, and use of many technological tools is prohibited. When speaking Low German, wearing distinctive clothing, or driving their horses and buggies along the roadways, the Older Order Mennonites choose a family life much different from their neighbours.

Second, Fatima Husain and Margaret O'Brien, from the University of North London in the United Kingdom, studied religion, family and community among Pakistanis in Britain. Using government statistics, research reports, and media information the authors show a changing pattern of family and community life. Religion has become more important to the Pakistanis in Britain as family and community ties to Pakistan have become weaker over time. The authors make suggestions for British governmental policy to assist Pakistani accommodation to the dominant culture. They also show the importance of religion to define values and to help families maintain a sense of community.

Third, Darren Sherkat of Vanderbilt University in the United States explores the work patterns of conservative Christian women. He starts with an analysis of widely circulated religious pamphlets and documents, finding that religious writers admonish women to care for their own young children. Dire consequences are predicted to ensue if the mother "abandons" her children to the care of others while she works outside the home. Sherkat then uses a longitudinal data set from the United States to see if in fact there is a link between religious conservatism and labour force participation of women. He finds that there is. Conservative Christian mothers of young children indeed are more likely than others to be out of the paid labour force and to be housewives. By the time children are grown, labour force participation of these women is similar to others. In the first three chapters, the authors remind us of the importance of religion in defining everyday life of families.

Fourth, Susan Ziehl, from Rhodes University in South Africa, chose English and Afrikaans speaking white families to study the effect of class and culture on household structure. Three hundred white respondents in Grahamstown, Eastern Cape Province, were surveyed. Research questions were designed to detect differences between these groups in value orientations and household structures. Further, the role of social class in these relationships is examined. Ziehl concludes that culture is a more important determinant of family structure than social class. Afrikaaners are more likely to live in extended families than English speakers are, although this is more likely among the lower than middle class is.

Fifth, Rachel Lawrenchuk and Carol Harvey, University of Manitoba, Canada demonstrate the effects of cultural loss and reclamation. In their qualitative research, participants show the negative effects of Canadian cultural policies on aboriginal families in the 1950s and 1960s. Through the voices of their participants, they explain the process of working with the dominant culture while reclaiming what had been lost from the Cree and Ojibway cultures.

Readers are invited to journey to these five locations with the authors of the chapters. By doing so, you can gain understanding of how minority families can maintain their differences from the dominant culture in which they live.

Series Editor's Preface

Emille Durkheim theorised modernity as a process of increased specialization, increased differentiation and, paradoxically, increased integration of the differentiated units for an upgraded adaptation of the social organism to its environment. Post-modernists argue that evolution is over and that we are witnessing a deconstruction: differentiation appears to be now in reverse gear not because of the fabled energy of what Durkheim called the *conscience collective* but because the increased access to knowledge-power axes effectively produce hybridity.

Globalisation under post-modern conditions is believed to be producing hybridisation and de-differentiation as youth of the world – be they Aboriginal Canadians, conservative Christian Americans, Pakistani Britons or Afrikaaner and English South Africans – are increasingly united in their taste for the same sorts of music, movies, clothes, gadgets and food, unless they are too poor to participate in the consumer society. It would seem to be the case that everything that is solid is melting into thin air as Marx and Engels prophesied at the height of the bourgeois modernist revolution.

The authors of the book indirectly beg to differ with people like Fukuyama who prematurely celebrate the triumph of the Anglo-American way. We do not quite live in a global village yet and there is every indication that liberal philosophy has not been bought by every culture in the multicultural world. This is because minority cultures still struggle to maintain their differences through the socialization of children and adults into family cultural traditions that are unique. Globalisation has not completely done away with differences due to the persistence of what some writers have termed the globalisation of apartheid. Given the perpetuation of social inequality in the New World Order, it is unlikely that minority cultures would completely let go of the slipping life-lines, changing identities, that give them a sense of location on the quicksand of history.

However, some of the minority cultures represented in this book are privileged minorities such as the Afrikanner and English communities of South Africa, conservative Christians in the US and old order Mennonites in Canada. What do these relatively privileged groups have in common with endangered cultures like Pakistanis in Britain and Aboriginal Canadians? The authors suggest that the answer is that all these minorities, though different, share a common interest in maintaining their differences from complete obliteration by the dominant cultures even while willingly sharing Levi Jeans, Coca Cola and Macdonalds with the dominant culture.

The authors note that the cultural struggles between minority and dominant groups take place in the context of public policy that is less likely to favour especially the previously unprivileged minority cultures. At the same time, all cultures, minorities included, are becoming more heterogeneous as a result of race-class-gender differences in religion, language, work, and the impacts of being a visible minority to be gazed upon.

The policy and theoretical implication of this book is that there is a need to study minority family patterns in an effort to discover lessons that majority groups could learn from minorities. Instead of assuming that the majority is always the norm into which the minority must be integrated and thereby basing policy and theory exclusively on the dominant, knowledge and policy could be advanced by also studying the minorities. Rather than celebrating the hegemonic values of the Durkheimian collective conscience, scholars and policy makers could benefit from a better knowledge of the less well-known family values of minorities, not just in terms of exotic recipes and ethnic music but more importantly, in terms of holistic child-rearing, health-caring, spiritual and labour relations.

- Biko Agozino
- Indiana University of Pennsylvania

1 The Old Order Mennonites: Application of Family Life Cycle Stages

JOHN E. PETERS

Introduction

The concept of family life cycle of the Old Order Mennonites (OOM), located in central Ontario, Canada is explored in this chapter. This analysis is appropriate for two fundamental reasons: The family is central in this culture, and children are significant to their family of orientation even beyond the years of their being launched. The OOMs have a unique way of socially and economically complimenting their grown children. The family life cycle approach to the study of the OOM is useful on three specific accounts. First, it gives us a better understanding of the OOMs. Second, it shows comparisons between the OOM and the more dominant modern and post-modern North American families in relation to stages in the family cycle in the present and the past. Third, it broadens our understanding of the family life cycle approach.

The focus of this study is upon a religious group of about 4,500 people now found in 15 church communities in several counties north and northwest of Waterloo, and in Mt. Forest, Ontario. This is the largest of five or six conservative groups who have their origins in Switzerland and Alsace, then migrated to Pennsylvania, and finally to Canada about 200 years ago. Their life style is apparent by the use of the horse and buggy, simple clothing, hard work, rejection of much of modernity, and the centrality of family and church.

The Family Life Cycle

The family life cycle approach to the study of the family was recognised as early as 1931. Its more contemporary use began in 1948 with eight specific stages (Duvall and Hill, 1948). The Duvall and Hill model has been modified by a number of scholars to account for such changes as divorce, remarriage, age, blended families, sole parenting, urban living and late parenting. Rodgers has expanded the family life cycle to 24 stages (1962). The family life cycle approach keeps the family as focus. Members interact with one another, and individuals as well as the family as a unit or organism change over time. Development is central and is anticipated. Roles and status change, often expanding through much of life, then contracting. This approach is centred upon the child (or children), which fits well in the OOM community. A fuller discussion of the family life cycle can be found in Duvall and Miller (1985, Chapters 1 and 2).

For our purposes of a conventional outline of the family life cycle in western societies, we refer to Duvall's model as indicated in Table 1.1.

Table 1.1 Eight Stage Family Life Cycle

1. Married couples (without children).
2. Childbearing families (oldest child birth – 30 months).
3. Families with pre-school children (oldest child 2 ½-6 years).
4. Families with school children (oldest 6-13 years).
5. Families with teenagers (oldest child 13-20 years).
6. Families launching young adults (first child gone to last child's leaving home).
7. Middle-aged parents (empty nest to retirement).
8. Ageing family members (retirement to death of both spouses).

Source: Duvall and Miller 1985, p. 26

In contrast, this paper will identify six stages of the family life cycle found within the OOM community. These are identified in Table 1.2.

1. Early Marriage

Husbands normatively marry between age 22 and 25 and wives between age 21 and 23. Marriages are endogamous and most likely from within the immediate geographical environs, a function of the focus of singings. The wedding is a major event, and is always held in the home of the bride's parents. (See Peters, 1987 for further discussion of weddings.)

The shift to the status of marriage is major in the OOM community. It contrasts sharply from the first stage of marriage in Western society in several areas. The couple really do not know one another very well. There is little opportunity for intimacy as is commonly practised among couples in the non-Mennonite community. On the other hand, this is a homogeneous society, and the variation in socialisation and experience found between OOM couples is minimal. They have spent little social time together with their peers, and minimal time separately as a couple. Very few violate the taboo of sex before marriage; therefore, one's first marriage means the initiation of sex. There is no honeymoon. Wives are not confronted with the tension of decisions relating to career and marriage. Marriage means carrying full responsibility for all domestic work and the imminence of childbirth and child rearing. Unlike many Western women entering marriage, she is knowledgeable of how to manage a household. She knows how to cook, bake, clean house, mend and make clothing,

Table 1.2 Old Order Mennonite Family Life Cycle Stages

Stage	Age	Commencement	Key characteristics
1. Early Marriage	21-26	Marriage	First intimacy
2. Childbearing	22-38	First child born	Birthing and raising children
3. Child raising	33-58	Last child born	Child and adolescent years
4. Launching	44-60	First child leaves	Children leave home
5. Daudy House years	60-80	Exit the family dwelling	New vocation for husband. Linkage with grandchildren, children, community
6. Restricting years	70+	Failing health	Assistance from others

in most cases efficiently. She knows how to attend to the needs of infants and children. She has augmented her understanding of these tasks by apprenticing in several homes in her late teen years. She is comfortable in working outdoors, taking full responsibility for the garden of vegetables and flowers as well as assisting in farm work with pigs, chickens and cattle. She has been socialised in her role from childhood, and particularly in her years since she left school at age 15 (see Peters, 1987).

As in her younger years, sexroles are clearly defined. The wife is a complement to her husband all her life. Her status in relation to her husband is further evident in that the new family unit is identified by her husband's first name: Aaron's, Edwin's, Daniel's. She will identify herself as: Mrs. Paul Martin, Mrs. John Weber. They are a couple, and only occasionally will she be engaged in any social activities apart from her husband.

Another marked contrast to the Western family, is that at marriage, should her parents be able, she will receive all furnishings for the house, including kitchen appliances, pots, dishes, furniture, bed sheets, up to eight quilts, and food for several days or weeks. This financial base at the time of marriage is unparalleled in Western society, except possibly in the upper class.

At marriage the husband immediately encounters an enormous economic responsibility. He will have purchased property, not rented an apartment as is the norm in Western society. More than 80 percent of OOM men have farms, and survive at least in part, by farming. Before his marriage he has very little capital. Until age 20 his father has garnished almost all the money he has earned either on the family farm or during his apprenticeship. After 20 he has been able to keep some of his earnings. (For tax purposes, in the past half dozen years parents have followed a different policy. They have put monies in trust to their child, and at the time of marriage this money is available to them in cash or kind). He may have his own horse and buggy, possibly a few pigs or beef cattle. The financial outlay to purchase and equip a 75-100 acre farm is between $200,000 and $400,000 US (the latter if one buys the milk quota for dairy farming at $10,000 US per cow). He operates in a community which makes this financial challenge surmountable. Parents strive to have finances (or land) available for this event, and some will mortgage their already paid farms to have money available. So as to make farming or some other career which complements the community's goals and values possible, his relatives, or senior members in the community will provide additional funds at very low interest rates. If there are non-relative lenders, one or two men will be designated to periodically check that farm decisions are made prudently.

The young husband works long hours to avoid any collapse of his investment. He knows that he will be a victim of market fluctuations in beef, hog, milk and even land prices. Like his wife in her domestic role, he has been well socialised in his farming role. As a boy of four and five he helped pick stones in the field. He helped with chores in the barn, was involved in seeding, harvesting and haying. The work ethic became part of his philosophy of life. As a teenager his responsibilities increased, and after his 15th birthday he became totally immersed in farming. Later he spent at least one year working on a farm other than that of his parents, apprenticing for his future role. He also learned some basic farm maintenance skills such as building, machinery repair, welding and harness repair. At marriage he catapults to his new role of farm ownership. To most in the Western family, this seems like a daunting task. In this new role he has community support. In this stage before child bearing, his wife assists in daily farm work, working along side her husband. She becomes fully acquainted with his work world.

2. Childbearing

This stage begins 10-16 months after marriage, sometimes a few months earlier or later. Birth control is seldom practised. Children are always welcomed and appreciated. Children reinforce the centrality of family in the OOM community. Childbirth is generally a two-day stay in the hospital. In recent years some have chosen to have home deliveries. The mother is likely to be assisted at home for a two-week period by a younger sister or maid. During a child's nursing years the mother becomes more confined to the house. Diapers and clothing are washed as necessary. Clothing is hung from the house (porch) upon the clothesline. On rainy days clothes are hung in two places: in the porch or over the kitchen wood stove which has a construct of four permanent two metre wooden rods extending some five centimetres parallel to the ceiling. Most kitchens have two stoves: wood (for winter, providing heat) and electric. OOMs use modern washers and spinners but no dryers.

For the next 15 years she is likely to bear more children at 14 to 36 month intervals. Appointments with a medical doctor are kept to a minimum because of costs. OOMs do not accept the social health plan of the province. It is possible for a physician in the hospital to be present at birth, and then not see this newly born again until she gives birth to a child 21 years later. With her third child she is likely to have permanent assistance with her domestic duties, a 16-20 year old woman. This maid will live-in and be involved in tasks from dawn to dark. Along with food preservation and preparation, the young mother will sew clothes for her children, and mend clothing for the family. Periodically she will entertain guests, a practice which is central within the larger Mennonite community. Families in their buggies may drive down the long lane of a farm after the Sunday church service without any earlier notice. The host's house is clean, and she has ample food for all.

While the father is conscious of needs for his wife and children, his energy is spent on the farm. A large number of farmers are dairymen, while others have a mixture of beef and hogs along with field crops. In the case of hogs and beef, trucks may come bimonthly to transport the animals to the local stock yards. The spring and fall seasons are especially busy with seeding and harvesting. He will also be engaged in other activities: helping others in corn harvesting, attending a sale of farm stock or used farm machinery, helping in barn raising, possibly donating a few days of farm labour to someone who has recently experienced an accident, or occasionally working with other men outside the community where a disaster like a cyclone or flood has occurred. In his vocation of farming he makes decisions whether to increase his herd or whether to expand his fields by renting more acreage. A few expand their activity by raising horses, welding or furniture making. This young farmer is conscious of making farm payments, while increasing his capital.

Pennsylvania Dutch is spoken almost exclusively in the home. Children encounter their first English environment in school, where only English is used, except for some assistance in the first few months. Where the school is beyond walking (or biking) distance, the father transports the children by horse and buggy. Upon return from school, children engage in chores. Until a child is 14 all travel together to church or for visits in the family buggy. (See Hiebert, 1998, for a portrayal of the life of OOM children).

By the time the children enter their teens, parents are aware that the time will soon come when they must have sufficient means to facilitate a son to begin farming or to engage in some other way of making a living. Every Mennonite family wants to make this provision for their children, a distinct ideal compared to Western families.

3.   *Child Raising*

Several aspects of this stage are a continuation of the second stage described above. Mothers bear children into their late thirties, and all the while nurture their offspring. During the day children find activity in the yard, barn or one of the sheds. There may be a swing from a tree, bicycles, a wagon or even a slide, as well as toy farm equipment in the sandbox. The all purpose living/dining room/kitchen with its large table serves as a place to play, read, and munch popcorn.

The child's understanding of the wider world is expanded, within boundaries, in the parochial school. The school pupil is identified as a scholar, who learns to read and write. Many take a particular interest in geography. History begins with the creation of Adam and Eve. Other crucial markers in history are Noah's ark, the time of Christ, Columbus' journey to America, the Reformation, the first immigration of Mennonites from the U.S. to Canada and the solidification of the more conservative lifestyle for OOMs in 1889. Students respect their teachers. Compared to discipline problems in the larger society, there are few among the OOM. Parents may become involved and almost always support the teacher. The lunch hour and recess periods are particularly active with both males and females participating in softball, skating, group games such as prisoner's base. This is the most gender integrated time of their entire lives. Girls wear long dresses, boys long pants. Upon their return from school they change clothes to do family and farm chores. Older parents tell me that the expectation of work for this generation of children is not as vigorous as it was in earlier years.

There is always a school Christmas program in which all participate. The size of two room schools necessitate two performance days with the grandparents attending the first afternoon, and parents the second. Songs and poems reinforce the values of the community: care and respect for one another, love of nature, regard for God. The second annual school event is a picnic on the second last day of school, with games and food on the school grounds.

In this stage I give more attention to the teen years, as it concerns both child and parent. Teenage children participate more in tasks and more responsibility in duties in the house and farm. In summer boys bike to a neighbour for an evening swim in the dugout. At age 14 he drives a horse and buggy to church accompanied by his younger siblings. Girls spend more time with those of her age cohort. A child's independence expands. At age 14 the child will continue attending school until the Christmas or Easter break. A few choose to terminate their schooling with the end of the school year. (In another conservative Mennonite community children quit school the day of their birthday.) They then assist with duties at home. They are now capable, mentally and physically, to do most of the tasks that are considered congruent to the OOM way of life, though some apprenticeship is necessary. Parents take this stage of development very seriously.

Girls learn the details of cooking, housekeeping and sewing. Her mother teaches her how to make her first and second quilt, a symbol as well as practical artefact in this culture, and a product that will be of great utility in her future.

Boys learn the care of domestic animals, seeding and harvesting, and the upkeep of buildings and equipment. He is likely to go to a relative or neighbour's farm to assist in times when additional help is needed. Almost all young people formally contract to apprentice in a home (women) or farm shop or construction team (men) for at least a year. This experience expands their understanding of domestic or agricultural life. They move in residence, and fully participate in the family life of their employer. Employers are not to exploit their hired help. At times a special bond is developed in this association, and at the time of marriage the former employer may make a special gift to the couple. By age 17 or 18 every male has his own buggy, and by age 19 his own horse, which arc given by his parents.

The management of money of OOM male youth is a unique practice. Parents take seriously the responsibility of establishing their son and daughter to a viable means of livelihood within the OOM culture. The cost of such an undertaking is enormous, particularly since most choose farming. By age 13 and 14 parents often have a sense whether their son will go into farming or some other vocation. They wish to be prepared for the day, at age 22-25, when he will step into that new role of being a self sufficient, as well as participant in the Mennonite community. The earnings of the employee always go directly to the father. He may return some money to his son or daughter, but he banks most of it so that it might be used as an accumulated gift at the time of marriage.

The Mennonite community has the least control over people in its constituency between age 16 and adulthood. Bonds with parents are not as strong, and contacts are made beyond that of the extended family, sometimes even beyond the Mennonite community. Young people do find time to be together. It may be an evening or Sunday afternoon playing volleyball, skating, or the guys may swim in a local dugout. Sports are not to be competitive, physical, nor costly in terms of equipment. Other activities on the local level might be a rock picking bee for some farmer who is handicapped, a comfort knotting bee, or pulling nails from used lumber. Prior to more modern machinery there was the corn husking bee. During these years it is likely that a group of young women or young men will make a distant trip to fellow Mennonites in the USA, such as in the states of New York, Pennsylvania or Indiana. Others will be braver and head for British Columbia or the Maritimes in Canada by either bus or train (not by aeroplane). Such activity is considered quite acceptable.

Singings are the conventional and acceptable young peoples' entertainment for both males and females, and are held almost weekly, on Sunday nights, beginning at about 8:00 p.m. Some may gather earlier for supper. Some 100 to 150 young people from the immediate area of two or three meeting houses (churches) meet in a home and sing hymns in four-part harmony. Young people begin frequenting singings at 15 years of age, the time when girls for the first time wear their long hair up. While most participate in the singing, a number of boys might meet outside or in the adjacent woodshed, and form their own entertainment. Young people sing until about 9:30 or 10:00, when couples leave. The remaining group engage in more singing, conversing and some square dancing. Baptised persons are expected not to participate in the dance.

Singings provide the forum in which young people can develop their ties with a partner who they might eventually choose as spouse. Young people initiate their couple relationship with letters. This is generally a very secret process, where few friends know about these exchanges. The first public event occurs when the young man with horse and buggy will pick up his girlfriend at the front door shortly after 9:30, at the end of a Sunday singing.

The couple drive to her home, where they enter the house and visit in the front room. Couples in a beginning relationship remain together until about midnight, and couples about to be married visit with one another until 2:00 in the morning. He then drives home, a distance of up to 12 kilometres. The next morning he is up at six doing the farm chores. A generation ago, the couple rarely conversed with one another, except on these singing occasions, or possibly a meeting of a smaller number of youth on Sunday afternoon.

OOM young people face an important decision between the ages of 17 and 19 which will effect them for the rest of their lives. This is the choice whether to make a commitment to the church, which really means a commitment to the community. Catechism classes supervised by the minister and bishop are held every summer for six consecutive Sundays. Interested young people terminate any deviant behaviour. Parts of the catechism (of 1632) are learned and pondered. The culmination is a baptismal service at which a commitment is made to God and the community. Rules of the community are read, and new members commit themselves to these regulations. This commitment is especially significant to men. At some future time, during their mature years, should they be called by the membership to serve as minister or deacon, and should they be chosen by lot, they agree to accept this responsibility, a position for which they do not receive any direct financial remuneration.

Parents and church leadership attempt to restrain the deviance of youth. Deviance very rarely involves the police. Deviance is most likely to be found among males. Periodically one or several may spend their time at the pub in the nearby village, absorbing the music or hockey game on TV. The more radical men find employment outside the community, purchase an automobile, and eventually leave the community, with its social and financial assets. Parents will continue having contact with him, but he will not fit into the sphere of financial and social benefits experienced by other OOM youth.

4.   Launching

Launching is a family affair with both social and economic dimensions. The obvious mark of launching is marriage. Banns are announced in the public meeting place three weeks in advance of the coming marriage. OOM take pride in making this announcement a surprise to the constituency. The wedding is commonly held in the bride's family's residence but never in the church. The impending wedding initiates a flurry of activity. The home where the wedding is held is thoroughly cleaned, and often the fences are freshly painted. A select group of some 100 to 150 persons are invited, and each considers it an honour to have been asked. Invitations are personally delivered by the couple. A generation ago, they were all hand-written. Along with the immediate families, the local preacher, bishop, uncles and aunts, a number of cousins and particularly intimate friends are invited. As people arrive by horse and buggy, four designated teenagers serve as hustlers, tending to the horses, and having them ready when the guests wish to depart. Similarly four female waitresses serve the head table of the wedding party and immediate family. Both hustlers and waitresses particularly appreciate the tips they receive, the sum being equally distributed among the eight participants. There is a fair degree of humour and jest in their activities. The two hour religious service which includes the actual marriage begins at 9:30. There is then a sumptuous meal, then a program of goodwill and humour, and most of the people over age 30 leave. The younger people stay for games. The couple spend their first night in a room upstairs. The second day they leave by horse and buggy to their new home.

In the launching process parents of the bride and groom are heavily engaged in many matters that facilitate the couple in their early marriage. Parents, siblings and possibly others assist in the renovations to buildings on the newly purchased property, and in the transport of stock and equipment to the farm. The parents of the bride do whatever they can to assist in making the home liveable and comfortable: cleaning and painting. If it is within their means they will supply all the furniture and appliances as well as pots, dishes and enough food for the couple through their first three weeks. The couple's beginning has been the focus of the parents' thoughts and actions for several years. Since OOM generally have between 5 and 8 children, the launching years may extend over several years and involve considerable time and finance. It is not uncommon for parents to make loans or mortgage their farm to assist in the launching of their offspring.

During the launching years parents enter the new role of grandparents. One obvious sign is that the grandfather now combs his hair forward rather than to the back or side. Grandparents are often the hub for visits from their married offspring and their children. At least once a year there is a gathering for all family members, at which time business matters may be discussed. Grandparents keep contact with their children, and periodically visit them, particularly the couples who have married in recent years. The grandparent role is recognised and respected by all grandchildren. Grandparents may move into the home of a married son or daughter to assist when particularly needed for several days. In such cases, both grandparents are present, not simply one, as might be the case in Western urban families.

5. Daudy House Years

Daudy means grandparent, and the move into the daudy house is a marked transition. The family farm is almost always acquired by the youngest son, at which time an extension to the house is built, and the parents move into it. In more recent years, sometimes a house trailer is simply attached to the original farm house. There is always a door between the two dwellings, sometimes a porch or causeway.

There is considerable variation when this transition is done. If there is only one son and he has three sisters after him, the parents are likely to be in their early fifties. If the son is the last child, the parents will be in their early sixties. In the event there are no sons, parents might sell the farm to one of their sons-in-law. In a few cases where elderly couples have no children, they may sell their farm to an interested young couple and take residence in the daudy house, identical to parents with children. In a few instances older couples move to a village where the husband finds day work. The elderly couple have the right to remain in this residence until their death.

The transition to the daudy house is most significant for the father. He relinquishes all financial involvement in the farm and seeks another means of income: day labour, a shop for woodworking or leather craft. His source of income drops considerably, but he has no thought but to facilitate his son. The financial arrangement is generally that the owner of the farm makes payments to his parents for the farm. The older couple, still capable of work, assist in daily chores, and at times care of the children, and in return they have free access to the garden and farm produce, as well as free use of their domicile until death. Young children readily access their grossdaudy's home, and are treated to special baking, and possibly bedtime stories. Grandparents facilitate the resident family by doing chores on the occasions when the married children are absent for business or some other late afternoon appointment. Grandmother sews, not only for the young children in the adjacent house, but also for other grandchildren. Relations between the two families is usually strengthened, but not always.

Moving into the daudy house marks the beginning of a decrease in responsibility. Their lifestyle is one wherein they may interrupt their work schedule for other engagements. This may be visits to family, friends, and those who are ill or restricted to their homes. They host guests who arrive unannounced for a visit. They make a point of attending funerals. A few make time to entertain or visit contacts they have established with OOMs in the USA. The Western age of retirement at 65 has no relevance among the OOM. They simply work and seemingly enjoy work as long as they are able.

6.   *The Restrictive Years*

OOM life is centred around family, Sunday worship and work. In the waning years of life, one's participation decreases due to failing health. One is no longer self-sustaining but assists in some farm or household activity which requires limited energy, whether outdoors or indoors. Mobility becomes restricted. They are no longer able to hook up their horse and visit others, but children and friends do make a point of making contact with them.

The OOM community care for the sick and elderly in a personable way. The community goes to great lengths to have those incapacitated comfortable in their own home. Should the immediate family be unable to take care of all the needs, a network of others will come to spend from eight to 12 hour shifts, to be present and to care. This may involve giving medication, assisting the person to exercise and walk, changing the bed sheets and other needs similar to that done in a hospital. In the event a person is hospitalised, the community makes great effort to visit the sick. If the immediate family cannot bear the expense for the elderly's housing and living, the large community of the 15 churches will assist. The elderly are not considered an inconvenience. They are looked after in the context of their natural living environment, in a manner that would be considered somewhat inconvenient for most Western families.

At death, a wake, and the funeral itself is held in the home. The casket is then ceremonially transported by horse and buggy to the cemetery and put to rest, followed by the funeral service with many in attendance. The cemetery is adjacent to the meeting house. While birth, the first event of life, is generally experienced in a hospital, the other two key events of marriage and death are recognised with appropriate jubilation and sobriety respectively, in the home.

Conclusion

The family life cycle approach is appropriately applied to the Old Older Mennonites. It does not have the extreme variation or deviation found in Western families. The "fit" of the family life cycle stages approach of the present OOM family is fairly congruent to the Western rural family at the turn of the century. One noticeable difference would be that Mennonites now experience an extended longevity compared to the general population a hundred years ago.

The OOM population has a focus upon children for an even longer period of time than that found in Western society. Similarly, because of the geographical proximity of extended family members, the family is central in a meaningful way in contrast to western families. Grandparents have a key role in at least three ways: They are visible, they are engaged with grandchildren, and grandchildren see grandparents while the former are interacting with parents throughout their developing years.

Life stages carry some distinct differences with Western society. Among the OOMs the first stage of being a couple without children is brief. The stages of childbearing and child raising are extended. The nature of the OOM child raising years generally has a lot more association between child and parents, where mother and father are present, compared to the dual earning urban parent. Children in Western families have much more exposure to extra-familial activity such as sports, music lessons, materialism and peer pressure. This preoccupation and force of socialisation is minimal among the OOMs. The launching years engage the parent with children in many social and practical ways. The daudy house years are unique in that fathers make major changes in vocation for their offspring, and both parents make minor changes in residence. Grandparents continue with a lot of contact with their children and grandchildren. In the restrictive years, Mennonite second-generation members are involved, a situation which few Western families experience. Seniors in Western families often prize their independent life styles.

The Old Order Mennonite family plays a central role in social, financial and religious activities virtually throughout one's total life span. One's identity is lodged in the family. To the OOM the family is distinctly central and is not substituted or compromised with profession, status mobility, economic security, travel, artistic preferences or academic curiosities, as is the case in many non-Mennonite Western families. The family life cycle approach adapts well to the Old Order Mennonite family.

References

Duvall, Evelyn and Hill, Reuben (1948), Co-chairmen, Report of the Committee on the Dynamics of Family Interaction. Washington D.C.

Duvall, Evelyn and Miller, Brent C. (1985), *Marriage and Family Development*, New York, Harper and Row.

Hiebert, Carl (1988), *Us Little People*, Boston Mills, Books, Erin Ont.

Peters, John F. (1987), Socialisation Among the Old Order Mennonites, *International Journal of Comparative Sociology*, Vol 28, 34, pp. 211-223.

Rodgers, R. H. (1962), *Improvements in the Construction and Analysis of Family Life Categories*, Ph.D dissertation, Western Michigan University, Kalamazoo.

2 South Asian Muslims in Britain: Faith, Family and Community

FATIMA HUSAIN AND MARGARET O'BRIEN

Introduction

With the continuous movement of peoples across national frontiers, fundamental problems have surfaced in the construction of new social boundaries and the structuring of families. For South Asian Muslim communities in Britain, the importance of faith, family and community continue to be a challenge in a secular and increasingly individualistic society. This chapter is a study of the Pakistani communities of Britain, which constitute its largest Muslim community and the third largest minority ethnic community after the South Asian Indian and Afro-Caribbean communities.[1] The first part of this chapter is a brief description of the migration of Pakistanis to Britain and their subsequent settlement. Second, we will examine social issues which have been at the heart of the adaptation and integration processes of South Asian Muslims to British society. These issues centre around family dynamics, including generational and gender differences and the creation of distinct ethnic-religious communities in Britain. Last, we will discuss Islamophobia and the creation of a new distinct identity, that of British Muslim. We will also draw on the research material and field work experience generated from a European Union funded project on Muslim Families in Europe: Social Care Provision.[2]

Although we mention South Asian Muslims and Pakistani Muslims as a group, it is important to note that various differences exist among diverse South Asian Muslim groups. The national-religious label, "Pakistani," often hides strong provincial, regional and kinship allegiances as well as distinct ideological and religious beliefs, the effects of rural/urban divide as well as class differences.[3]

Migration to Britain

In the case of Pakistanis the initial out-migration flow was of men for economic reasons and was part of a wider flow of migrants to fill the labour shortages in post-war Europe. The movement of workers from Pakistan followed the general pattern of migration from Commonwealth countries to Britain and remained unrestricted until 1962. Migration was also limited by geographical regions. The majority of British Pakistani (95%) are from a specific number of rural districts and villages, mostly in the Punjab and the North East (Dahya, 1973). By far the largest group is from the Mirpur district in Azad Kashmir in the North East.

As was often the case, an extended family, kin group or village in Pakistan would pool resources to send one male member to Britain, who in his turn would regularly send part of his earnings back home to be distributed among the kin or family group. This trend of migrants originating from a limited number of geographical areas is a consequence of strong kinship ties which led to additional male migrants being sent to Britain as soon as the family/kin group had enough resources for an additional passage to Britain

The 1962 UK immigration law ended the automatic entry of Commonwealth citizens to Britain. Henceforth, entry was limited to those who had work vouchers or children under 18 years of age. As a result, the number of adolescent boys entering Britain to work alongside their fathers, brothers or other male relatives grew significantly. At this stage, the migration of women (mostly wives) was taking place at a very slow rate, and the predominance of male Pakistanis in Britain continued for over a decade. Male migration kept the traditional family and kinship-ties strong, with male workers returning to Pakistan every few years for extended holidays to get married, to participate in weddings and other family events. The final intention behind this flow of male migrants was that, eventually, they would return home to their extended families and that their younger male relatives would replace them in Britain and continue sending remittances home (Dahya, 1973). Further immigration restrictions in 1971 ended the migration of single men and shifted the emphasis to family reunification by permitting wives and children to enter together as dependants of male workers. Consequently, the proportion of Pakistani women in Britain increased significantly from 15% of the Pakistani population in 1961 to nearly 50% in 1981 (Nielsen, 1992).

Prior to 1991, population data were collected based on nationality and with increasing numbers of Pakistanis obtaining British citizenship, data on the number of Pakistanis in Britain were rather imprecise. The 1991 Census was the first in Britain to gather data on ethnic self-definition as well as nationality. The data showed that out of a minority ethnic population of 3 million (5.5% of the population of GB), 476,600 were of Pakistani origin (0.9%) (Table 2.1).

Table 2.1 South Asian Populations of Great Britain

Ethnic Group	Great Britain (thousands)	Percentage
White	51,873.8	94.5
All Ethnic Minorities	3,015.1	5.5
South Asian	1,479.6	2.7
Indian	840.3	1.5
Pakistani	476.6	0.9
Bangladeshi	162.8	0.3

Source: National Ethnic Minority Data Archive, Owen (1992).

Table 2.2 Regional Distribution of Pakistanis in Britain (four most densely populated areas)

Region	Total Population (000s)	Population of Pakistanis (000s)	%
Greater London	6,679.7	87.8	1.3
West Midlands MC	2,551.7	88.3	3.5
West Yorkshire	2,013.7	80.5	4.0
Greater Manchester	2,499.4	49.4	2.0

Source: National Minority Date Archive, Owen (1994).

While the Indian communities of Britain constitute the largest ethnic minority, it is difficult to measure the proportion of Muslim Indians because statistics are collected on ethnicity but not on religious affiliation. However estimates made in a survey by Modood, et al., (1997) indicate that 96% of Pakistanis, 95% of Bangladeshis and only 6% of Indians in Britain are Muslim. In the late 1990s, Muslims along with other religious groups successfully lobbied for the inclusion of a question on religious self-identification in the next British census which will take place in 2001.

The majority of Pakistanis coming to Britain were economic migrants and consequently their destination in Britain was, for the most part, the industrialised urban heartland of England. By far the majority of Pakistanis (64%) settled in the Greater London area or the industrialised centres of the West Midlands, Yorkshire and the North West. The Pakistani communities of Britain are concentrated in Birmingham, Bradford, Manchester and Luton (Table 2.2).

Constructing Communities

The migration of women and children attenuated the influence of the wider transnational extended family, but emotional and economic ties to the family or kin group in Pakistan were not severed. The kinship ties maintained by Pakistanis to their family networks in Pakistan are still stronger than those maintained by other South Asian communities in their country of origin (Ballard, 1990). However, with the arrival of families the myth of an eventual return to the homeland ended conclusively and traditional family structures were transformed.

Families that were reconstructed in Britain were for the most part nuclear in nature. The economic hardship of establishing a home in Britain and supporting additional family members led to fewer resources being sent to the family back to Pakistan. Economic hardships also led some women into paid employment, usually as under-paid home workers, but employment rates were lower than national levels for all women. A 1994 survey found that 70% of Pakistani women were economically inactive (homemakers) and only 15% were full time workers, compared with 37-39% of white women (Modood, et al., 1997, p.86). For Bangladeshi women, traditionally having fewer educational and language skills, the stay at home rate is 81% with only 6% in full time employment. However, many of the economically inactive women may actually be involved in homeworking (Modood, et al., 1997), an activity which has not been recorded. Ballard (1996, p.135) states:

Many Pakistani women are involved in homeworking, most usually by stitching up clothing for local manufacturers.

As the number of Pakistani families in Britain increased, the need to create communal structures and establish social cohesion became more urgent. The creation of a distinct social and cultural world centres for Muslims around the limitations set by religious belief with boundaries defined by the divine entity in the Qur'an (*Hudud Allahi*). The formation of different Pakistani Muslim communities was possible due to the concentration of Pakistani families in a limited number of urban areas and by the continuation of transnational arranged marriages, often with cousins (Lewis, 1994). While Sikhs and Hindus are barred from marrying close kin, Muslims are permitted and often encouraged to do so. This has led Pakistanis to create self-contained and somewhat closed and isolated communities based on an extensive system of inter-related members, while Hindus and Sikhs have had to look outwards to non-related community members to create social and cultural structures.

The other fundamental aspect in the creation of a cohesive Pakistani Muslim community has been the local mosque. Initially established in residential houses, mosques have provided not only a place of worship but also a meeting place to discuss social issues. Additionally, the mosques have been the centre of necessary religious education for children being brought up in Britain. The mosque, as a focal point along with locally established small businesses owned by Muslims providing halal meat and other provisions as well as the perpetuation of kinships ties, has led to the formation of distinct communities.

In Britain, community mosques often reflect the provincial, linguistic and ideological distinctness of different Muslim communities. For example, mosques may be differentiated provincially by being "Mirpuri" or "Kashmiri," linguistically by the language spoken by the Imam, and ideologically by sectarian differences. This patterning of religious-cultural differentiation may disappear with the loss of provincial and national identification by younger generations of Muslims who may also require English speaking Imams. Sectarian differences may persist but there has been no documentation of either common cross-sectarian worship or the number of mosques distinguished by ideology (i.e. Shia, Sunni, Ahmedi and other minority Muslim sects).

Along with the establishment of community mosques, an overlapping development of branches of South Asian Islamic movements has also taken place. Three large Sunni movements present in Britain are: the Ahl-i-Hadith which controls over a dozen mosques and is centred in Birmingham, the Jamaat-i-Islami which has established the Islamic Foundation, a centre for research and publishing outside Leicester (Nielsen, 1992) and the Tablighi Jamaat which is less structured but whose members frequent most Sunni mosques. The agendas of some of these large movements is politico-religious in nature and aims to establish a modern Muslim community protected from Western moral and ethical corruption.

Field work on the EU project has shown that the image, function and ideological basis of some local community mosques may be changing due to the influx of recent refugee groups (Husain and O'Brien, 1999).[4] While there have been cultural shifts within the Muslim communities and familial structures and social networks are being transformed, the mosque remains a symbol of continuity, stability and cohesion. Werbner (1996, p.115), states that the mosque is not only a communal meeting place and a place of prayer but also

> The base for teaching collective discipline, organisation, and internal fundraising, the springboard for regional and national political alliances, and a training ground in polemics and adversary politics.

However, the mosque for all its communal functions remains a male dominated space with access to women limited normally to one specific area of the mosque, if not prohibited all together. This gender based spatial patterning is effective in excluding women from all discussion and decision making that takes place and isolating them by not permitting access to the communal power structures centred at the mosque.

Socio-economic Concerns

Economically, Pakistani communities continue to be more disadvantaged than other ethnic minority communities. The unemployment level for Pakistani men is twice that of white men (34% to 17%) and in some urban areas it is over 42% (Modood, Beishon and Virdee, 1994). Economic hardships along with discriminatory structures have led to various problems within the community, not least are those of changing gender roles and male disempowerment due to loss of status and honour as the family breadwinner.

Gender relations defined by traditional patriarchal laws and religious dictates of prescribed social roles have created the general impression of inflexibility and oppression. While British society has shown a lack of understanding of traditional gendered roles shaping Muslim women's lives, Muslim communities themselves are undergoing constant change as they try and adapt to living as a minority in Britain. South Asian Muslim women have also been challenging the *status quo* established by traditional Muslim communities, but their social adaptation and change is hindered by many factors.

If the principles of citizen's rights and gender equality have not been understood by Pakistani women, it is not because these ideas are non-existent in their society of origin but because most of these women are from rural areas and many have had no formal education. Language and communication difficulties compound the problems women face, most evident for older Pakistani women. The rate of fluency in English among 45-65 year old Pakistani women is 28% and rises to only 47% for 25-44 year olds (Modood et al., 1997, p. 61). The lack of formal education and fluency in English has had an impact not only on the understanding of women's rights but also on their access to health and social services. Apart from providing advice and assistance, many women's organisations have been trying to strengthen the position of women in the community by developing literacy and English skills classes with the aim of enabling women to speak publicly and act on their own behalf (Burlet and Reid, 1998).

Our study of access to social services has clearly shown that the lack of proper interpreters and the use of male family members as interpreters has led to many problems being hidden by the families and the community as a whole (Husain and O'Brien, 1999). Recent anecdotal indications are that domestic violence is on the rise and some South Asian women's refuges report that the majority of their users are Muslim women. [5] However, it is still unclear whether domestic violence is indeed on the rise or whether this trend reflects a heightened awareness among South Asian Muslim women of their rights and an increase in confidence in claiming those rights based on an increase in reported rates. One, idea, as yet unresearched, is that the loss of control over the economic well-being of the family has led men to vent their frustrations on their immediate family members.

Additionally, social isolation, marital problems along with economic deprivation have led to high rates of depression among women. In one small scale study conducted at a local doctor's office centred in an area with a high proportion of Pakistanis in Manchester, 60% of presenting women between 22-24 (out of a sample of 56 women and 21 males) showed symptoms of depression (Husain, Creed and Tomenson, 1997, p. 434). Furthermore, South Asian women are reported to have a raised suicide rate, and research has shown that 75% of

South Asian women seen by a doctor following deliberate self-harm had marital problems (Merill and Owens, 1986).

However, problems in accurate diagnosis are prevalent not only due to communication problems arising from a lack of fluency in a common language but also due to different perceptions of mental health and well-being. It has been suggested that movement towards a more holistic approach including religious and spiritual dimensions as well as taking into account the experience of being a minority may help in correct diagnosis and proper treatment.

Community living steeped in patriarchal traditions does not assist women in obtaining information on their rights as citizens. Male resistance to change in family structure is often the root of the problem. In our study, social workers in a small town in Oxfordshire stated that community elders, all male, had attempted to close down a women's advice centre opened in a predominantly Pakistani neighbourhood by lobbying the local council to cut the centre's funding. Currently, the centre is under threat of closure. A social worker of Pakistani origin working in the area stated that the problem is of male dominance: "Men don't want their wives to go for help independently because they [men] want control" (Husain and O'Brien, 1999).

However, not all is so bleak as has been demonstrated by Pakistani women in Bradford in 1995. An incident involving police and Pakistani youth escalated to a confrontation between riot police and a group of about three hundred men after a meeting with community representatives did not resolve the situation. Tempers were calmed by a group of multi-ethnic women (Pakistani and white) who placed themselves between the protesting crowd and the riot police (Burlet and Reid, 1998).

This action taken by women brought to the forefront gender relations and community representation. Some accused the community representatives of responding in a manner "typical of an elite trying to hold on to a power base that was no longer guaranteed" (Burlet and Reid, 1998, p. 281). According to Burlet and Reid (1998, p.283), after this incident women became more determined to express their opinions, demanding decision making power and self-representation and stating that:

> The vast majority of community leaders are male and many are conservative in outlook, they do not adequately represent the full range of community members.

While the majority of males cling to their traditional hegemony and appropriate the voice of the community, presenting "an image of internal harmony and enclosed culture within communities..." (Burlet and Reid, 1998, p. 273), changing attitudes are manifested not only among women but also among the British born younger generations.

New Identities

Changes among Pakistani youth have taken place at the level of self-definition and are a reflection of their separation from the parental generation and their disillusionment with the process of integration and social acceptance. The questioning of identity has also led to a distinction being made among ethnicity, religion and nationality.

The issue of nationality is the easiest to resolve. Since the majority of youth are by birth or naturalisation British citizens and their allegiance to Pakistan as a nation is steadily fading, the label British is not a contested identifier. Whether one is British Pakistani or British Muslim is a difficult discussion, particularly when the boundaries of where ethnicity ends and religion begins is unclear.

For the born in Pakistan parental generation identifying themselves as Pakistani, the religious elements are subsumed in the ethnic label. This conflation of ethnic and religious identities is also a reflection of Pakistani political nationhood which is based on the idea of a South Asian Muslim homeland. In the perception of the younger generation of Pakistanis who may have only spent short periods of time in Pakistan and who have no memory of the struggle for independence against British rule, the call for a Muslim homeland, and the suffering of partition, the notion of being Pakistani is separate from that of being Muslim.

However, religion remains a strong force in the lives of the majority of Pakistanis. When asked to respond to the question, "Religion is very important to how I live my life," 73% of Pakistanis and 76% of Bangladeshis concurred, while only 13% agreed in the white ethnic group (Modood, et al., 1997, p. 308). While the importance of religion is apparent, it is difficult to assess what percentage of younger Muslims have turned to traditional orthodoxy and what proportion take a more pragmatic approach to belief and practice.

The distinction between ethnicity and religion is based on the separation of a place of socio-cultural origin which is geographically fixed and the *ummah* or Muslim community which has a specific place of origin but has no geo-political boundaries. This separation of identities has a strategic function in family issues and youth revolt.   Although the younger generations recognise and identify themselves with a place of origin, that is, they continue to maintain ethno-geographical group allegiances (Beishon, Modood, and Virdee, 1998, p. 383), they have rejected parental attachment to an ethno-religious identity as being based in superstitions and traditions.   Often their rejection of parental traditions has taken them not towards Western mores which would lead to communal alienation but to a religious doctrine cleansed of cultural impositions. The move toward true Islamic teachings has enabled many women to resist parental restrictions on education, freedom of movement and ideas around arranged marriages.   The younger generations functioning beyond the kinship and communal social spaces and boundaries of their parents have encountered Muslims from different cultural backgrounds, which has enabled them to separate religious dictates from traditional cultural practices.

The idea of belonging to a community removed from human intervention is also attractive at a social level.   The disenfranchisement and alienation of Pakistani youth in Britain is a concrete reality to which solutions have not been found.   Structural racism, the impotence of community elders in influencing political processes and effectively addressing socio-economic problems, and lack of political representation, have made the idea of a global community which can perhaps regain its former power, an attractive proposition.

Politico-religious movements such as the Jamaat-i-Islami have been taking advantage of this alienation by forming youth groups and addressing socio-political alienation.   Other extremist groups such as the Khilafa movement which advocates separation and a return to a caliphate have also managed to gain attention and support not only in Britain but also in other European nations.[6] These groups while providing a base of resistance and hope remain highly ideological and have yet to provide solutions to concrete socio-economic problems faced by Muslim communities.

This movement towards a religious identity which supersedes national and ethnic allegiances is not entirely a monster from the outside as the West had tended to depict it, but is in part a reflection of the constant prejudice and discrimination against visible minority ethnic individuals and Muslim minorities that is perpetuated by the majority ethnic community.   Widespread prejudice against Islam and Muslims in Britain has been highlighted by a recent report by the Runnymede Trust (1997, p.11) on what the authors identify as Islamophobia:

A deep dislike of Islam is not a new phenomenon in our society. What is new is the way it is articulated today by those sections of society who claim the mantle of secularism, liberalism and tolerance.

While Islamophobia shapes collective responses which in turn influence global politico-religious movements, the diversity within Muslim communities is ignored and deemed irrelevant. Not only are minority ideological beliefs often disregarded but also the historical heritage and rich cultural traditions of ethnic groups is rejected for a globalisation of religious belief. This globalisation, one could state, will perpetuate cultural traditions based only not on the Qur'an but on Arab society in the Arabian peninsula during the time of the Prophet. In fact in this process or struggle, many liberal Muslim voices are silenced and others become unwitting defenders of "Islamic" practices and policies which they do not support.

Conclusion

The settlement of Pakistanis in Britain over the past 50 years began as a movement of workers, but with the arrival of families the myth of return to the homeland finally ended. Pakistani communities began to recreate communal structures as a minority in a highly individualised society with alien traditions and values. In this paper we have shown that being a minority has led to many communities maintaining protective rigid boundaries marked by their ethnicity, culture, religious and linguistic backgrounds.

Until recently, the response of British society had been defensive. Up until the late 1990s, within government and political and cultural institutions there has been a strong tendency to view Pakistani cultures and traditions as pathological. Clearly, there has been a failure to grasp the differences and the rich heritage of the various Pakistani communities. Additionally, a lack of foresight in perceiving the internal changes that have been taking place within the communities in Britain is apparent and has resulted in lost opportunities to capitalise on the economic and political potential of a dynamic ethnic group.

There are, however, some optimistic signs of possible cultural shifts. Apart from the report on Islamophobia, the Runnymede Trust has issued a consultation document and establish a Commission on the Future of Multi-Ethnic Britain which will record the responses to the document. Additionally, certain South Asian Muslim writers have been at the forefront of current debates on issues, such as the Salman Rushdie affair and whether the education of Muslims should be separate or integrated into mainstream education.[7] They have been voicing the concerns of Muslim communities in Britain, irrespective of religious or political affiliations.

Most importantly, change is evident within some sectors of the new Labour government. In 1998, The Home Secretary, the Rt. Hon. Jack Straw MP met with representatives of British Muslim communities and signalled the need for issuing guidance to criminal justice agencies to take into account the need to protect Muslims (Statement following a meeting between the Home Secretary and a Delegation from the Muslim Council of Britain, Home Office Press Release, June 16, 1998).   A significant change on the part of the Muslim delegation was the inclusion of a member of the minority Shi'a sect.[8]   The government's willingness to consider change will, one hopes, have a significant impact on the general perception of Muslim communities in Britain.

Apart from these few changes, the ignorance of not only the average British citizen but also of academics and politicians about Islam and the diversity of Islamic beliefs and practices continues. This ignorance and the lack of sustained political will to make changes across Europe and other industrialised countries has given momentum to a global movement and an identity which is aware of its victimisation and is steadily becoming politicised and confrontational. These failures on the part of the ethnic majority have had a profound impact on Pakistani, Muslim, and visible minority ethnic communities not only in Britain but also within the European Union.

Recent political changes in Britain, namely, the devolution of the Scottish, Welsh and Northern Ireland parliaments, are having a significant impact on the perception of identity (individual, social and political) and will pose further challenges to the concept of essentialist, ossified cultures. It is becoming increasingly apparent in Britain that there is no fixed majority ethnic culture, nor is there a static definition of Britishness. In particular, as the Scottish begin a process of political self-determination and carve out their own distinct identity, discussions have taken place on what it means to be British as well as English. While the debate on separating Englishness from Britishness, two identities which had become fused, continues, new questions have risen regarding the place of minorities within new nationalistic boundaries. For instance, can one be a Scottish Asian?

Although British society is beginning a process of re-thinking the identity question and British Pakistani communities are still in the process of change, redefining familial structures and negotiating identities, it appears that European societies as a whole still remain fixed in their preconceptions of atavistic cultural differences.[9] A Pakistani activist in Denmark has aptly stated that integration is not a one way street and if treated as such it will never succeed (Husain and O'Brien, 1999). Individually and collectively, we should be involved in a process of mutual integration shifting away from essentialist definitions of family, culture and belief and towards a recognition of fluid spatial boundaries and overlapping cultural spaces creating a more hybrid (Beishon, et al., 1998) society of re-negotiated non-essentialist identities.

Notes

1 We will refer to the Bangladeshi community specifically where appropriate.
2 This research project was sponsored by Directorate General V of the European Commission and was conducted in collaboration with non-profit organisations in Belgium, Denmark and the UK.
3 Although Pakistani is a nationalistic label there is a religious sub-text to it because of the Hindu-Muslim conflicts in pre-partition British India and the eventual creation of the nation state Pakistan (1947) for the Muslims of India.
4 One local North London and one London mosque have become the final destination for young political refugees from Algeria. Their presence has successfully alienated the traditional South Asian congregations and modified the mosques into a hostel/cafe/places of worship.
5 This information was obtained during informal discussions with the Asian Women's Resource and Help Centre (ASHA) based in Lambeth, London.
6 After the death of the Prophet in 632 the spiritual and political leadership of the Islamic state was taken over by the first orthodox Khalifa and companion of the Prophet. The first schism took place at the Khalifa's appointment with the Shi'a appointing 'Ali as the spiritual successor of the Prophet. The caliphate continued in one form or another until the end of the Ottoman empire.
7 For over a decade, academics and writers such as Professor Tariq Modood (University of Bristol) and Yasmin Alibhai-Brown (IPPR, London) have been discussing South Asian identities and religious identity within Britain.
8 The inclusion of minority voices is significant since one of the weaknesses of the innovative Islamophobia report was the lack of minority representation in the membership of the commission writing the report.
9 It is important to note that the integration process has distinct implications in different European states and that there is great variance in attitude towards ethnic minorities from one European state to another. However, at the same time, Muslim communities (settled and refugee) in a majority of European countries have become the specific targets of anti-immigrant campaigns by far right and mainstream political parties.

References

Alibhai-Brown, Y. (1998), Islam and Euro-Identity. *Eurovisions: new dimensions of European Integration*, Demos Collection 13, pp. 38-40.

Ballard, R. (1990), Migration and Kinship: the differential effects of marriage rules on the process of Punjabi migration to Britain in C. Clark, C. Peach and S. Vertovec (eds). *South Asians Overseas: Migration and Ethnicity*, CUP, Cambridge, pp. 219-249.

Ballard, R. (1996), Negotiating race and ethnicity: Exploring the implications of the 1991 Census, *Patterns of Prejudice*, vol. 30, no. 3.

Beishon, S., Modood, T. and Virdee, S. (1998), *Ethnic Minority Families*, London: Policy Studies Institute.

Brah, A. (1987), Women of South Asian Origin in Britain: Issues and Concerns, *South Asia Research*, vol. 17, no.1, pp. 39-54.

Burlet, S. and Reid, H. (1998), A Gendered Uprising: political representation and minority ethnic communities. *Ethnic and Racial Studies*, vol. 20, no. 2, pp. 270-287.

Dahya, B. (1973), Pakistanis in Britain. *New Community*, vol. 2, no. 1, pp. 25-33.

Husain, F. and O'Brien, M. (1999), *Muslim Families in Europe: Social Existence and Social care*, report for EU-DGV, University of North London, London.

Husain, N., Creed, F. and Tomenson, B. (1997), Adverse Social Circumstances in People of Pakistani Origin in the UK, *British Journal of Psychiatry*, vol. 171, pp. 434-438.

Lewis, P. (1994), *Islamic Britain*, I.B. Tauris Publishers, London.

Merrill, J. and Owens J. (1986), Ethnic Differences in Self Poisoning: a comparison of Asian and White groups, *British Journal of Psychiatry*, vol. 148, pp. 708-712.

Modood, T., Beishon, S., and Virdee, S. (1994), *Changing Ethnic Identities*, London: Policy Studies Institute.

Modood, T., Berthoud, R., Lakey, J., Nazlioo, J., Smith, P., Virdee, S., and Beishon, S., (1997), *Ethnic Minorities in Britain: Diversity and Disadvantage*, London: Policy Studies Institute.

Nielsen, J. (1992), *Muslims in Western Europe*, Edinburgh UP, Edinburgh.

Owen, D. (1992), Ethnic Minorities in Great Britain: Settlement Patterns, *1991 Census Statistical Paper 1*, NEMDA, University of Warwick, London.

Owen, D. (1994), South Asian People in Great Britain: Social and Economic Circumstances, *1991 Census Statistical paper 7*, NEMDA, University of Warwick, London.

Runnymede Trust (2000), Islamophobia: a challenge to us all (1997), London. *Social Trends, vol. 30*. The Stationary Office, London.

Statement Following a Meeting Between the Home Secretary and a Delegation from the Muslim Council of Britain (June 16, 1998), Home Office Press Office, London. Website: www.homeoffice.gov.uk

Werbner, P. (1996), The making of Muslim dissent: hybridized discourses, lay preachers, and radical rhetoric among British Pakistanis, *American Ethnologist*, vol. 23, no. 1, pp. 102-122.

3 "That they be Keepers of the Home": The Effect of Conservative Religion on Early and Late Transitions into Housewifery*

DARREN E. SHERKAT

Introduction

Feminist critiques of religion invariably cite the patriarchal tendencies of the Christian tradition - pointing to passages from sacred texts and influential theological tracts that place women in a divinely sanctioned subordinate role (Brown and Bohn, 1989). Indeed, sociologists have demonstrated a link between fundamentalist orientations and affiliations and inegalitarian gender role attitudes (Hughes and Hertel, 1987; Peek et al., 1991). A few scholars have investigated the connection between women's labour force participation or occupational attainment and religious affiliation, finding that non-religious women and those from non-conservative backgrounds are more likely to be in the labour force or have elite careers (Bainbridge and Hatch, 1982; Chadwick and Garrett, 1995; Hertel, 1988; Lehrer, 1995). However, no study has analysed panel data to investigate the effects of religious beliefs on women's career choices. Generally, social scientists have tended to neglect unpaid home labour as a career option despite its prevalence, continued persistence in the face of increasing female labour force participation, and its consequences for other outcomes such as: marital happiness and divorce (Schoen and Urton, 1979; Trent and South, 1989); social psychological dispositions (Shehan, Burg, and Rexroat, 1986); and fertility (McLaughlin, 1982; Smith-Lovin and Tickmeyer, 1978). Social scientists have paid considerable attention to the consequences of exit from the paid labour force for marriage and the family, the economic factors that lead to female participation in the paid labour force (Brinton, Lee, and

29

Parish, 1995; Oppenheimer, 1973), and the economic contributions of housewives to the household (Berheide, Berk, and Berk, 1976; Oppenheirmer, 1977). Yet, few have investigated the social forces that might lead women to choose to become a housewife (an exception is Ridgeway, 1978).

Recent examinations of the influence of fundamentalist Protestant orientations on educational attainment have reinvigorated interest in the material consequences of culture (Darnell and Sherkat, 1997; Glass, 1998; Lehrer, 1999; Sherkat and Darnell, 1995). A flurry of research in the 1960s and 1970s attempted to link religious culture to stratification (Glenn and Hyland, 1967; Gockel, 1969; Goldstein, 1969; Lenski, 1961; Schuman, 1971). However, this enterprise failed largely because of a lack of understanding of religious cultures (Greeley, 1964; Stryker, 1981). The Catholic-Protestant differences touted by Weberians simply did not pan out in a national context where Catholics have extremely diverse ethnic and socio-economic origins, and where Protestantism runs the gamut from the world-affirming deistic agnosticism of the liberal "mainline" to vividly other worldly hell-fire-brimstone conservative sects. Indeed, feminist critiques of Christian patriarchy also lack sufficient specificity because of the diversity of religiously motivated gender role orientations (Bartkowski, 1997). By focusing on a set of religious groups with similar and clearly defined prescriptions and proscriptions regarding education, gender roles, and lifestyle, it is possible to identify distinctive cultural influences on stratification. Fundamentalist Protestantism provides the necessary ingredients.

Using written materials widely circulated in conservative Protestant communities, I document how conservative Christians view female labour force participation - proscribing careers other than that of housewife, especially when children are in their "tender years." To test whether these religious prescriptions and proscriptions influence women's decisions to become a housewife, I examined data from the Youth Parent Socialization Panel Study (Jennings, Markus, and Niemi, 1991). Since career transitions are dynamic, I modelled both entry and exit from housewifery using survival regression analysis (Kalbfleisch and Prentice, 1980) and multinomial logistic regression (Agresti, 1990). My findings reveal some interesting time-dependent relationships between fundamentalist religious orientations and becoming a housewife. First, early transitions to becoming a housewife were strongly influenced by fundamentalist orientations. Second, inerrantist beliefs in the Bible did not predict transitions to becoming a housewife later in the early life course. Third, fundamentalist orientations significantly increased the risk that a woman spends her early career as a housewife, and then enters paid employment later in life.

These findings attest to how fundamentalists view women's roles and careers, and how female fundamentalists negotiate their familial and religious commitments in an economic climate that necessitates paid employment.

Women's Roles and Fundamentalist Christianity

For many fundamentalist Protestants, women's roles are of paramount concern. The divine order of family relations relies on the headship of a Christian husband, the submission of the wife to her husband, and the subordination of children to their parents. Without this pattern of authority, many conservative Christians believe that the family cannot function properly, and a host of personal and social problems will proliferate. The theological basis for female subordination in the Christian tradition has three key foundations - all rooted in a literal interpretation of sacred texts. First, the order of creation in the myth of Genesis is often pointed to as a justification for male domination. "For man was not made from woman, but woman from man. Neither was man created for woman, but woman for man" (1 Corinthians 11). Second, Christians often trace women's subordination to the fall from grace - since Eve defied God's order, all women are cursed (Brown and Bohn, 1989). Third, women's relegation to household duties is anchored in Paul's letter to Titus (2:3-5), where he admonishes women to: "teach the young women to be sober, to love their husbands, to love their children. To be discreet, chaste, keepers at home, good, obedient to their own husbands, that the word of God be not blasphemed." The implication is clear - to go against the will of the husband or to take up activities outside of the home is a violation of God's law. Some conservative Christians argue that submission in marital relationships should be mutual for husband and wife, and social scientists who study conservative Christian family relations have long noted that power in the family is considerably nuanced (Bartkowski, 1997; McNamara, 1985). However, conservative Christian religious groups continue to affirm the requirement of female submission. This was most recently evidenced in the passage of the Southern Baptist Convention's *Faith and Message* statement on the family, which argues that, "A wife is to submit graciously to the servant leadership of her husband even as the church willingly submits to the headship of Christ."

A whole genre of conservative Christian literature touts the domestic role of women. Writers admonish housewives to let Christ or the Holy Spirit guide all of their actions, and submission to the husband is equated with submission to

God. Indeed, one classic book of this genre, Maxine Hancock's (1975) *Love, Honor, and Be Free*, begins with the thesis "Resolved, that woman's place is barefoot, pregnant, and in the kitchen." After expressing some hostility to the proposition, Hancock builds her entire book around it, arguing that the freedom of the housewife and submission to God and husband make being barefoot, pregnant, and in the kitchen the best possible choice for a woman's happiness. Submission to God and husband also involves subordinating "selfish" interests in career, sexuality, and self-fulfilment for the needs of the family—particularly the children (Hancock, 1975; Horton, 1982; Jepsen, 1988; LaHaye, 1976, 1980). This has led many conservative Christian writers to advocate the subjugation of economic interests for the sake of the family. For example, Marilee Horton (1982:15) writes: "The conclusion that I have come to is that God would have me encourage young Christian mothers to choose to be keepers of the home, to take care of their children and to trust God to take care of their financial and other needs." Women who work outside of the home while their children are young are seen as the root cause of divorce, infidelity, juvenile delinquency, teen pregnancy, pornography, homosexuality, and male unemployment (Hancock, 1975; Horton, 1982; Jepsen, 1988; Lahaye, 1976, 1980). Further, conservative Christian writers characterise working mothers as unhappy, unfulfilled, libertines destined for loneliness and failure. Indeed, conservative Christians consider the childless feminist the most aberrant and unhappy person. One oft mentioned example in this literature comes from the author Taylor Caldwell from *Family Weekly*:

> There is no solid satisfaction in any career for a woman like myself. There is no home, no true relationship, no hope, no joy, no expectation for tomorrow, no contentment. I would rather cook a meal for a man and bring him his slippers and feel myself in the protection of his arms than have all the citations and awards and honours I have received world-wide, including the ribbon of the Legion of Honour, and my property, and my bank accounts (reprinted in Horton, 1982, Schlafly, 1977, and elsewhere).

For conservative Christian women, the most important thing that they can be is a wife and mother. Many of the recent texts on the joys of being a housewife mention a quote attributed to Golda Meir that "having a baby is the most fulfilling thing a woman can ever do."

Interestingly, I found little evidence that writers found women incapable of holding careers. All of the authors professed that women were just as capable as men for most jobs. Indeed, Christian women are encouraged to seek careers if they desire, once their children are grown (Horton, 1982; Jepsen, 1988). Horton explains:

> In the Garden of Eden, God didn't tell Eve that she couldn't eat fruit; she could have it all—all but one. Satan convinced her that the reason God didn't want her to eat that one was because it was the best. She obeyed his urging to "do her own thing." It wasn't the end of Eve, only the end of God's perfect plan for her life, and she took us all down with her. The Feminists are not wrong about women being just as intelligent, capable, and creative as men, but I believe they are cheating many women out of God's perfect plan for their lives by urging them to grab the wrong apply first.

Such statements emphasise social scientists need to understand fundamentalists' religious commitments from the point of view of these religious actors (Bartkowski, 1997; McNamara, 1985). Conservative Christians are not loath to women in the workforce, but instead are articulating opposition to mothers of young children in the workforce.

My reading of conservative Protestant "insider documents" leads to three hypotheses about the relationship between fundamentalist Christian orientations and becoming a housewife:

1. Women who believe that the Bible is the inerrant word of God will be more likely to become housewives.
2. Inerrantist women will become housewives earlier in life, and will be more likely to remain housewives.
3. Conservative Christian women will be no less likely to re-enter the paid workforce once they have fulfilled their motherly obligations in the "tender years."

Data

To examine transitions into and out of being a housewife I used data from the Youth Parent Socialisation Panel Study (YPSPS) (Jennings, et al., 1991). The first wave of the YPSPS was completed in spring of 1965 and yielded interviews with 1,669 high school seniors, 99% of those targeted by the study. A randomly selected parent of each child was also interviewed, resulting in 1,562 interviews with parents (93% of those contacted). In 1973 the second retained 1,348 (80.8%) of the students from the original panel, and 676 were women. The third wave was conducted in 1982, when the second generation respondents were about 34 years old. Interviews were completed by 1,135 of the original respondents (68%), 566 of them with women.

Transitions into and out of Housewifery

Respondents were asked what their occupation was in 1973 and in 1982. In 1973, 208 women, 30.8% of the sample, reported being a housewife. In 1982, 159 women, 28.1% of the sample, reported their occupation as housewife. Of the 1973 housewives, 73 (35%) reported being a housewife in 1982, while 135 (65%) of the housewives from the 1973 panel reported some other occupational status (most in the paid labour force, along with a few students). Between 1973 and 1982, 86 women (15% of the total) became housewives. Respondents were not asked how long they had been a housewife; however, two timing variables can be constructed for examining rates of becoming a housewife: (1) timing the event from the age of marriage and, (2) timing the event by the woman's age at the birth of her first child. It is not possible to use YPSPS data to answer specific questions about the timing and ages of children and becoming a housewife or leaving housewifery, and a woman could also have more than one child influencing her occupational choices.

Biblical Inerrancy

In the 1965 and 1973 panels respondents were asked: "I'd like you to tell me which is closest to your own view: (1) The Bible is God's word and all it says is true; (2) The Bible was written by men inspired by God, but it contains some human error; (3) The Bible is a good book because it was written by wise men, but God had nothing to do with it; and (4) The Bible was written by men who lived so long ago that it is worth very little today." Since biblical inerrancy is a key feature of Christian ideologies that support becoming a housewife, I constructed a dummy variable identifying those who chose the first response. If a woman did not become a housewife between 1965 and 1973, her score on biblical inerrancy was allowed to change to the 1973 value for predicting transitions between 1973 and 1982.

Participation in Protests

The countercultural movements of the 1960s and 1970s had a significant effect on career and family trajectories of activists, and Sherkat and Blocker (1997) found that activists were unlikely to become housewives. I constructed a dummy variable distinguishing respondents who participated in the anti-war, student, or civil rights protests of this era.

College Preparation and Educational Attainment

Students indicated the type of curriculum they were pursuing in high school: college preparatory; vocational, general, business, agricultural, or other. I created a dummy indicator for college preparatory course-work to assess the effects of such preparations on becoming a housewife. Preliminary analyses showed that the effect of education on the likelihood of becoming a housewife is non-linear. Graduation from college reduces the likelihood of becoming a housewife, but there were no differences between women with only high school education and some college, or between women with undergraduate versus graduate degrees. I constructed a dummy indicator flagging women who did not graduate from college.

Income

The likelihood of becoming a housewife may be influenced by a woman's earning potential and/or the household income of her family. I examined the relationship between transitions to becoming a housewife and both household and personal income in 1973 and 1982.

Social Origins

I controlled for the effects of mother's education. The measure runs from (1) primary school education, to (7) graduate degree. I also used dummy indicators to control for rural and Southern origins.[1]

Methods

I begin by comparing means for four groups of women: (1) Those who never reported being a housewife; (2) those who reported being a housewife in both 1973 and 1982 ("Stable housewives"); (3) those who reported being a housewife in 1973 but not in 1982 ("Transitory housewives"); and, (4) those who were not housewives in 1973, but were in 1982 ("Late housewives"). After comparing these means, I constructed accelerated failure time models of transitions to becoming a housewife based on the bivariate results.   (The relatively small number of cases necessitates paring down the number of independent variables in the analyses.) I present results from models where the timing of becoming a housewife is calculated from the age of marriage and from age of first birth. Preliminary analyses showed that for both indicators of the timing of becoming a housewife the best fitting distribution of the hazard is the log-normal model (Kalbfleisch and Prentice, 1980; Miller, 1982). This specification of the hazard takes into account that transitions are a non-monotonic function of age, with low rates of transition early in the earliest years, higher rates of becoming a housewife in the early 20s, and then declining rates later in the early life course. Exponentiated coefficient estimates from these survival models can be interpreted as an impact of a one unit change in an independent variable on the rate of transition to becoming a housewife (Kalbfleisch and Prentice, 1980; Sherkat, 1991).   Finally, I examined multinomial logistic regression models examining the effects of covariates on the odds of being a stable housewife, transitory housewife, late housewife, and never a housewife.   Exponentiated coefficients from these models represent estimated effects of a one-unit increase in an independent variable on the odds of making one occupational choice versus a comparison occupation (Agresti, 1990).

Results

Table 3.1 examines differences between *stable house*wives (women who reported being a housewife in both 1973 and 1982), *late housewives* (women who reported being a housewife in 1982 but not 1973), *transitory housewives* (women who identified themselves as housewives in 1973 but not in 1982), and *non-housewives* on a variety of covariates.   Looking first at religious differences, Table 3.1 shows that biblical inerrancy is much more common among women who became stable housewives compared to women who were late housewives or who never became housewives. However, fundamentalists were not significantly more likely to become stable housewives than to become transitory housewives. Further, women who subscribed to biblical inerrancy were significantly more likely to become transitory housewives than to never be a housewife.

Table 3.1   Means on Independent Variables for Stable Housewives, Late Housewives, Transitory Housewives, and Never Housewives

	Stable Housewives 1973-1982	Late Housewives 1982 only	Transitory Housewives 1973 only	Never Housewives
Southern	.219	.198	.222	.234
Rural	.603	.360^b	.363^c	.390^c
College-Track Curriculum	.247	.570^c	.356^e	.516^{ch}
Mother's Education	2.672	2.804	2.644	2.821
Education in 1973	1.452	2.012^c	1.519^f	2.081^{ci}
Education in 1982	1.616	2.116^c	1.704^f	2.304^{ci}
Personal Income in 1973	3.446	6.815^c	3.575^f	6.863^{ci}
Personal Income in 1982	2.669	2.835	4.778^{be}	7.123^{cfi}
Family Income in 1973	11.283	12.036	11.657	11.576
Family Income in 1982	12.551	14.370^b	12.754^e	13.381^d
Protested 1965-1973	.000	.093	.067	.154^{ch}
Biblical Inerrancy	.521	.337^a	.400	.267^{ch}

a = difference from Stable Housewife significant at .05 level.
b = difference from Stable Housewife significant at .01 level.
c = difference from Stable Housewife significant at .001 level.
d = difference from Late Housewife significant at .05 level.
e = difference from Late Housewife significant at .01 level.
f = difference from Late Housewife significant at .001 level.
g = difference from Transitory Housewife significant at .05 level.
h = difference from Transitory Housewife significant at .01 level.
i = difference from Transitory Housewife significant at .001 level.

Of course, the religious differences reported in these bivariate results could be a function of a host of demographic and socio-economic factors that are associated with fundamentalist religiosity but causally related to women's occupational options.   First, women who grew up in rural areas were significantly more likely to become stable housewives, though they were about equally represented in the other three groups. Educational attainment was lower among stable and transitory housewives. However, late housewives and those who never reported being a housewife have similar levels of educational attainment. Personal income differences were largely a function of labour force exit, so it is not surprising that non-housewives (at whatever time point) earned more. It is somewhat revealing that there were no family income differences between the four groups in 1973.   Importantly, late housewives enjoyed significantly higher family incomes in 1982 compared to every other group. Additionally, protesters were significantly less likely to become housewives in their early 20s, and biblical inerrancy has been shown to significantly reduce the odds of participating in the protests (Sherkat and Blocker, 1994; Sherkat, 1998). Indeed none of the former protesters reported that her occupation was housewife in both 1973 and 1982. Yet, enough protesters became housewives by 1982 that their proportions among late housewives and never housewives were not significantly different.

The empirical results of Table 3.1 and preliminary analyses suggest a clear distinction between early and late transitions into and out of becoming a housewife, and this necessitated a piecewise analysis of the time series (Namboodiri and Suchindran, 1987). Table 3.2 presents results from two sets of log-normal survival regression models for transitions to early housewifery. I present two sets of models, one calculating the timing of becoming a housewife from marriage, the other using the birth of a woman's first child. The result from each set of models are almost identical. Controlling for other factors, including education and participation in the protests of the 1960s and 1970s, my estimates reveal that beliefs in the inerrancy of the Bible significantly increased the hazard of becoming a housewife between 1965 and 1973. When the timing of housewifery was calculated from the age of marriage, my estimates predicted that inerrancy boosts rates of becoming a housewife by 15% (exp. (.144) =1.15). Estimated effects of inerrancy on the hazard of becoming a housewife were somewhat lower when timing was calculated from first childbirth. Inerrancy increases rates of becoming a housewife by 9% in the final model (exp. (.084)=1.09). Hence my estimates suggest that in any given year for the first eight years after high school, young women who believed that the Bible is the inerrant word of God in high school are between 9-15% more likely to exit the labour force to become a housewife, controlling for other factors.

Table 3.2 Log-Normal Survival Regression Models of Becoming a Housewife by 1973

	Timing Calculated from Marriage		Timing Calculated from First Birth	
	Par. Estimate *Standard Err.*	Par. Estimate *Standard Err.*	Par. Estimate *Standard Err.*	Par. Estimate *Standard Err.*
College Prep.	-.087[c]	-.026	-.064[d]	-.023
	(.028)	(.029)	(.019)	(.019)
Southern	-.063[b]	-.048	-.035	-.025
	(.032)	(.032)	(.021)	(.021)
Rural	.008	.001	.001	-.003
	(.027)	(.026)	(.018)	(.017)
Mother's Education	.012	.007	.003	.000
	(.013)	(.013)	(.008)	(.008)
Family Income 1973	-.002	-.003	.001	-.000
	(.004)	(.004)	(.003)	(.003)
No College Degree		.213[d]		.142[d]
		(.040)		(.027)
Protested	-.128[b]	-.081	-.075[b]	-.043
	(.053)	(.053)	(.035)	(.035)
Biblical Inerrancy	.169[d]	.144[d]	.100[d]	.084[d]
	(.029)	(.028)	(.018)	(.018)
Intercept	3.484	3.391	3.411	3.347
Normal Scale Par.	.265	.257	.176	.171

[a] p< .05 one tailed.
[b] p < .05 two tailed.
[c] p < .01 two tailed.
[d] p < .001 two tailed.

Table 3.3 Multinomial Logistic Regression comparing Stable Housewives, Late Housewives, Transitory Housewives, and Never Housewives

	Stable vs Never	Late vs Never	Transitory vs Never	Stable vs Never	Late vs Never	Transitory vs Never
College	-.944[c]	.187	-.450[b]	-.463	.255	-.010
Preparation	(.307)	(.256)	(.223)	(.323)	(.282)	(.232)
Southern	.728[b]	-.306	-.548[b]	-.655[a]	-.289	-.467[a]
	(.333)	(.315)	(.261)	(.338)	(.315)	(.266)
Rural	.647[b]	-.131	-.338	-.599[b]	-.143	-.388[a]
	(.275)	(.255)	(.221)	(.277)	(.256)	(.222)
Mother's	-.011	-.044	-.107	.022	-.039	-.071
Education	(.128)	(.123)	(.105)	(.128)	(.124)	(.106)
Family	-.039	.324[b]	.098	.074	.329[b]	.130
Income	(.164)	(.158)	(.130)	(.164)	(.158)	(.131)
No College				1.787[d]	.161	1.399[d]
Degree				(.556)	(.289)	(.333)
Biblical	1.236[d]	.537[a]	1.330[d]	1.097[d]	.518[a]	1.185[d]
Inerrancy	(.286)	(.279)	(.227)	(.289)	(.282)	(.232)

Note: standard errors in parentheses
[a]p < .05 one tailed.
[b]p < .05 two tailed.
[c]p < .01 two tailed.
[d]p < .001 two tailed.

Participation in the protests significantly decreased rates of becoming a housewife; however, controls for educational attainment eliminated the significance of this effect. Likewise, taking college preparatory courses in high school significantly reduced the risk of becoming a housewife by 1973, though controls for educational attainment wipe out the significance of this effect. Finally, having no college degree by 1973 significantly increased the hazard of becoming a housewife, boosting the likelihood by 15-24% per year (exp. (.142) -1.15, exp. (.213) -1.24) controlling for other factors.

While the results of the survival models are instructive, they do not allow a complete comparison of the predictors of transitions into and out of becoming a housewife. Since the duration of being a housewife is unknown in these data, competing risks or multiple transition models cannot be estimated (Kalbfleisch and Prentice, 1980). However, multinomial logistic regression models allowed me to predict the net effects of covariates on the odds of becoming a stable, transitory, late, or late housewife versus never being a housewife, and to compare the effects of covariates on the odds of being in one housewife category or another. Table 3.3 presents these findings comparing the three housewife categories to never being a housewife.[2]

Biblical inerrancy dramatically increased the odds of being a stable or transitory housewife versus never being a housewife, controlling for all other factors. Compared to others, Bible believers were around three times as likely to be stable or transitory housewives than non-housewives (exp. (1.097) = 3.00 for stable versus non-housewives, exp. (1.185) = 3.27 for transitory versus non-housewives), when other factors were held constant. Fundamentalist women were also somewhat more likely to be late housewives than never to become housewives.

As in the survival models, educational attainment also helped explain becoming a housewife. Women who did not attain a college degree (or did not prepare for college in high school) had significantly higher odds of becoming a stable housewife or transitory housewife compared to never being a housewife. Interestingly, there were no educational differences between late housewives and non-housewives. Further, controlling for other factors, family income boosted the odds of being a late housewife versus never becoming a housewife. Additionally, women who grew up in rural areas had significantly higher odds of becoming a stable housewife versus never being a housewife.

Table 3.4 presents the multinomial logistic regression estimates comparing covariate effects on transitions into stable versus late housewifery, and transitory versus late housewifery. The estimates show that biblical inerrancy significantly increased the odds of being a stable housewife versus becoming a late housewife, though controls for education reduced the significance of this effect to below conventional levels. Further, fundamentalist women had significantly higher odds of being transitory housewives versus late housewives, and controls for educational attainment did not erase the significance of this effect. Biblical inerrantists compared to non-inerrantists had almost twice the odds of being a transitory housewife compared to becoming a late housewife (exp. (.667) = 1.95), when other factors were held constant.

Table 3.4 Multinomial Logistic Regression comparing Stable Housewives and Transitory Housewives to Late Housewives

	Stable vs. Late	Transitory vs. Late	Stable vs. Late	Transitory vs. Late
College	-1.132[c]	-.637[b]	-.718[a]	-.266
Preparation	*(.367)*	*(.299)*	*(.390)*	*(.325)*
Southern	-.422	-.242	-.367	-.178
	(.419)	*(.362)*	*(.422)*	*(.365)*
Rural	.788[b]	-.206	.742[b]	-.244
	(.341)	*(.298)*	*(.342)*	*(.299)*
Mother's	.033	-.063	.061	-.032
Education	*(.163)*	*(.145)*	*(.163)*	*(.145)*
Family	-.285	-.226	-.255	-.198
Income	*(.209)*	*(.181)*	*(.208)*	*(.183)*
No College			1.627[c]	1.238[c]
Degree			*(.599)*	*(.401)*
Biblical	.700[b]	.793[c]	.579	.667[b]
Inerrancy	*(.357)*	*(.311)*	*(.362)*	*(.315)*

Note: Standard errors in parentheses
[a] p < .05 one tailed.
[b] p < .05 two tailed.
[c] p < .01 two tailed.
[d] p < .001 two tailed.

College preparatory coursework significantly reduced the odds of becoming a stable or transitory housewife versus a late housewife. Controls for educational attainment eliminated the significance of the effect of college preparation on the odds of being a transitory versus a late housewife, but a marginal negative net effect of college tracking on being a stable versus a late housewife remained. Educational attainment significantly decreased the odds of being a stable housewife versus becoming one later in life. Further, educational attainment decreased the likelihood of making an early transition into and out of housewifery versus becoming a housewife later in life. Rural residents were significantly more likely to become stable housewives than late housewives, controlling for other factors.

Discussion

The reasons for women's exit from the labour force have too often been explained in purely economic terms, or by vague appeals to tradition and socialisation. In this paper, I have attempted to identify a particular cultural foundation that motivates the decision to become a housewife. By examining fundamentalist insider documents, I have shown how conservative Christian's view women's roles, and particularly women's labour force options and decisions. These cultural orientations are sustained in tight knit communities and reinforced through strict socialisation (Ellison and Sherkat, 1993a, 1993b). In the end, my results show a considerable effect of fundamentalist beliefs on women's labour force participation. These effects follow a particular logic, and are not uniform over the life course. Fundamentalist women are not simply averse to participation in the labour force. Indeed, fundamentalists themselves do not militate against women working, but instead argue that women should "put the home first." While fundamentalist women are significantly more likely to choose the home as their career in their early life course, I have also found that fundamentalist women are likely to re-enter the workforce when their children are older.

Future research should continue to take seriously cultural motivations for occupational choices. Indeed, the finding that more educated women are likely to become housewives later in life - especially net of family income - may well reflect an upper-class cultural motivation for housewifery. Still, much more needs to be sorted out in the interdependencies of time-related processes such as marriage, fertility, educational attainment, and labour force entry and exit. For example, religious factors have a considerable influence on marriage and marital relations, both the timing of marriage and the likelihood of divorce (Call and Heaton, 1997; Hammond et al., 1993), and both marriage and religious factors also influence fertility (Lehrer, 1996; Thornton et al., 1992). Both educational attainment and marriage likely have a reciprocal effect on one another, and religious factors have also been shown to influence educational attainment (Darnell and Sherkat, 1997; Glass, 1998; Lehrer, 1999; Sherkat and Darnell, 1995, 1999). And of course, all of these factors are going to influence women's transitions into and out of being a housewife. Recent methodological advances are making the modelling of such complex relationships possible; however, data limitations hamper the application of these methods of testing sociological theories.

Notes

* This chapter was previously published in *Review of Religious Research* (2000), vol. 41: 3, pp. 344-358. It is reprinted here with permission.
1 One reviewer noted that it would help elucidate the relationship between religious beliefs and commitments and women's labour force exit if it was possible to also investigate the influence of religious factors on gender role ideologies. Unfortunately, there are no measures of gender role ideology available until the 1973 panel of the study. Rather than violate the temporal order to assess the effects of gender role ideology on labour force exit, I have assessed the influence of both religion and becoming a housewife on gender role ideologies and changes in beliefs about gender roles in a separate paper (Sherkat et al., 1994).
2 Unfortunately, since no protesters were stable housewives in the YPSPS, coefficients for the effect of protest on transitions into and out of becoming a housewife cannot be estimated.

References

Agresti, Alan (1990), *Categorical Data Analysis*, New York: Wiley.
Bainbridge, William Sims and Hatch, Laurie Russell (1982), Women's Access to Elite Careers: In Search of a Religion Effect. *Journal for the Scientific Study of Religion* 21:242-254.
Bartkowski, John P. (1997), Debating Patriarchy: Discursive Disputes over Spousal Authority among Evangelical Family Commentators, *Journal for the Scientific Study of Religion*. 36:393-410.
Berheide, Catherine White, Berk, Sarah Fenstermaker, and Berk, Richard A. (1976), Household Work in the Suburbs: The Job and Its Participants, *Pacific Sociological Review* 19:491-518.
Brinton, Mary C., Lee, Yean Ju, and Parish, William L. (1995), Married Women's Employment in Rapidly Industrialising Societies: Examples from East Asia. *American Journal of Sociology*. 100:1099-1130.
Brown, Joanne Carlson and Bohn, Carole R. (1989), *Christianity, Patriarchy, and Abuse: A Feminist Critique*. New York: Pilgrim.

Call, Vaughn R. and Heaton, Timothy B. (1997). Religious Influence on Marital Stability. *Journal for the Scientific Study of Religion.* 36:382-392.

Chadwick, Bruce A. and Garrett, H. Dean (1995), Women's Religiosity and Employment: The LDS Experience. *Review of Religious Research.* 36:277-293.

Darnell, Alfred and Sherkat, Darren E. (1997), The Effect of Protestant Fundamentalism on Educational Attainment. *American Sociological Review.* 62:306-315.

Ellison, Christopher G., and Sherkat, Darren E. (1993a), Conservative Protestantism and Support for Corporal Punishment. *American Sociological Review.* 58:131-144.

Ellison, Christopher G., and Sherkat, Darren E. (1993b), Obedience and Autonomy: Religion and Parental Values Reconsidered. *Journal for the Scientific Study of Religion.* 32:313-329.

Glass, Jennifer (1998), The Impact of Childhood Fundamentalism on Women's Adult Socio-economic Attainment. Paper presented at the annual meetings of the American Sociological Association.

Glenn, Norval D., and Hyland, Ruth (1967), Religious Preference and Worldly Success: Some Evidence from National Surveys. *American Sociological Review.* 32:73-85.

Gockel, Galen L. (1969), Income and Religious Affiliation: A Regression Analysis. *American Journal of Sociology.* 74:632-647.

Goldstein, Sidney (1969), Socioeconomic Differentials among Religious Groups in the United States. *American Journal of Sociology.* 74:612-631.

Greeley, Andrew M. (1964), The Protestant Ethic: Time for a Moratorium. *Sociological Analysis.* 25:20-33.

Hammond, Judith A., Cole, Bettie S., and Beck, Scott H. (1993), Religious Heritage and Teenage Marriage. *Review of Religious Research.* 35:117-133.

Hancock, Maxine (1975), *Love, Honor and Be Free.* Chicago: Moody Press.

Heaton, Tim B., Jacobson, Cardell K., and Fu, Xuan Ning (1992), Religiosity of Married Couples and Childlessness. *Review of Religious Research.* 33:244-255.

Hertel, Bradley R. (1988), Gender, Religious Identity and Work Force Participation. *Journal for the Scientific Study of Religion.* 27:574-592.

Hertel, Bradley and Hughes, Michael (1987), Religious Affiliation, Attendance, and Support for Pro Family Issues in the United States. *Social Forces.* 65:858-882.

Horton, Marilee (1982), *Free to Stay at Home: A Woman's Alternative.* Waco: Word Books.

Jennings, M. Kent and Markus, Gregory (1984), Partisan Orientations over the Long Haul: Results from the Three-wave Political Socialisation Study. *American Political Science Review.* 78:1000-1018.

Jennings, M. Kent, Markus, Gregory, and Niemi, Richard J. (1991), *Youth Parent Socialisation Panel Study 1965-1982.* Computer File. Inter-University Consortium for Political and Social Research, Ann Arbor, Michigan.

Jepsen, Dee (1988), *Women: Beyond Equal Rights.* Waco: Word Books.

Kalbfleisch, John D. and Prentice, Ross L. (1980), *The Statistical Analysis of Failure Time Data.* New York: John Wiley and Sons.

LaHaye, Beverly (1976), *The Spirit Controlled Woman.* Eugene: Harvest House.

LaHaye, Beverly (1980), *I am a Woman by God's Design.* Fleming H. Revell.

Lehrer, Evelyn (1995), The Effects of Religion on the Labour Supply of Married Women. *Social Science Research.* 24:281-3301.

Lehrer, Evelyn (1996), Religion as a Determinant of Marital Fertility. *Journal of Population Economics.* 9:173-196.

Lehrer, Evelyn (1996), Religion as a Determinant of Marital Fertility. *Journal of Population Economics*. 9:173-196.

Lehrer, Evelyn (1998), Forthcoming. Religion as a Determinant of Educational Attainment: An Economic Perspective. *Social Science Research*.

Lenski, Gerhard (1961), *The Religious Factor*. New York: Doubleday.

McLaughlin, Steven D. (1982), Differential Patterns of Female Labour-Force Participation Surrounding the First Birth. *Journal of Marriage and the Family*. 44:407-420.

McNamara, Patrick H. (1985), The New Christian Right's View of the Family and Its Social Science Critics: A Study in Differing Presuppositions. *Journal of Marriage and the Family*. 47:449-458.

Miller, Rupert. *Survival Analysis*. New York: John Wiley and Sons.

Mueller, Charles W. (1980), Evidence on the Relationship between Religion and Educational Attainment. *Sociology of Education*. 53:140-152.

Namboodiri, Krishnan and Suchindran, C.M. (1987), *Life Table Techniques and their Applications*. New York: Academic Press.

Oppenheimer, Valerie Kincade (1973), Demographic Influence of Female Employment and the Status of Women. *American Journal of Sociology*. 78: 946-961.

Oppenheimer, Valerie Kincade (1977), The Sociology of Women's Economic Role in the Family. *American Sociological Review*. 42: 387-406.

Oppenheimer, Valerie Kincade (1997), Women's Employment and the Gain to Marriage: The Specialization and Trading Model. *Annual Review of Sociology*. 23:431-453.

Peek, Charles W., Lowe, George D., and Williams, L. Susan (1991), Gender and God's Word: Another Look at Religious Fundamentalism and Sexism. *Social Forces*. 69: 1205-1221.

Ridgeway, Cecilia L. (1978), Predicting College Women's Aspirations from Evaluations of the Housewife and Work Role. *Sociological Quarterly*. 19:281-291.

Schlafly, Phyllis (1977), *The Power of Positive Woman*. New Rochelle: Arlington House.

Schoen, Robert and Urton, William L. (1979), A Theoretical Perspective on Cohort Marriage and Divorce in Twentieth Century Sweden. *Journal of Marriage and the Family*. 41: 409-415.

Schuman, Howard (1971), The Religious Factor in Detroit: Review, Replication, and Reanalysis. *American Sociological Review*. 36:30-46.

Sewell, William H. Jr. (1992), A Theory of Structure: Duality, Agency, and Transformation. *American Journal of Sociology*. 98:1-29.

Shehan, Constance L., Burg, Mary Ann, and Rexroat, Cynthia A. (1986), Depression and the Social Dimensions of the Full-time Housewife Role. *Sociological Quarterly*. 27:403-421.

Sherkat, Darren E. and Blocker, T. Jean (1997), Explaining the Political and Personal Consequences of Protest. *Social Forces*. 75: 1049-1076.

Sherkat, Darren E., Blocker, T. Jean, and Steib, Kelley (1994), Gender Attitudes over the Life Course: An Examination of the Determinants of Gender-role Preferences and Preference Change. Paper presented at the annual meetings of the Southern Sociological Society, Raleigh, N.C.

Sherkat, Darren E. and Darnell, Alfred (1995), Gender, Religion, and Educational Attainment: Exploring how Inerrantist Orientations Influence Women's Life Chances. Paper presented at the annual meetings of the Society for the Scientific Study of Religion, St. Louis, MO.

Sherkat, Darren E. and Darnell, Alfred (1999), The Effect of Parents' Fundamentalism on Children's Educational Attainment: Examining Differences by Gender and Children's Fundamentalism. *Journal for the Scientific Study of Religion.* 38: 23-35.

Sherkat, Darren E. and Ellison, Christopher G. (1997), The Cognitive Structure of a Moral Crusade: Conservative Protestant Opposition to Pornography. *Social Forces.* 75: 957-982.

Smith-Lovin, Lynn and Tickamyer, Ann R. (1978), Nonrecursive Models of the Labour Force Participation, Fertility Behavior and Sex Role Attitudes. *American Sociological Review.* 43: 541-557.

Thornton, Arland, Axinn, William G., and Hill, David H. (1992), Reciprocal Effects of Religiosity, Cohabitation, and Marriage. *American Journal of Sociology.* 98:628-651.

Trent, Katherine and South, Scott J. (1989), Structural Determinants of the Divorce Rate: A Cross-Societal Analysis. *Journal of Marriage and the Family.* 51:391-404.

4 Class, Culture and Household Structure – A View from South Africa

SUSAN C. ZIEHL

Introduction

The question of the role of class and/or culture in explaining family diversity has most frequently been posed with reference to the United States (Allen, 1979; Tienda and Angel, 1982; Zinn and Eitzen, 1990). The debate has been about whether differences in the household patterns characteristic of blacks (African-Americans) and whites are best explained with references to socio-economic factors or cultural predispositions. In other words, do material conditions prevent certain sectors of society from achieving the household structures they desire or are household structures the product of cultural ideals held by individuals across the socio-economic spectrum? This debate is also of relevance to other societies. For instance, extended family living is a far more common feature of the family life experiences of black as opposed to white South Africans and the question can be asked as to whether this is related to the very stark differences in the socio-economic status of these communities and/or to differences in the emphasis placed on collectivism and individualism in African and Western cultures.

The purpose of this chapter is to present two models of the relationship between class, culture and household structure which derive from the author's own research into the family patterns of an ethnically divided white South African community as well as a consideration of the findings of American and other South African studies relevant to this topic.

Some American Studies

Allen's (1979) analysis of U.S. census data on households revealed that there are both ethnic/racial and class differences in the propensity to live in particular

49

household types. Conventional family structures (two-generational and headed by a married couple) are more common among whites than blacks and in the higher as opposed to lower socio-economic categories. Contrary to expectations, Allen did not find that extended families *per se* were substantially more common in the lower than upper socio-economic categories (1979). However, black families were found to be significantly more likely to be extended than white families. One of the ways in which Allen explains these findings is by pointing out that there is a relationship between "headship" and "extendedness" and contends that since black families are more likely to be female-headed, they are also more likely to be extended. With regard to his main analytical question (role of class and culture in explaining variations in household structure), Allen favours the "class-side" of the debate claiming that it is because black Americans are better represented in the lower socio-economic categories that they are also more likely to live in extended family households. More recently, Zinn and Eitzen have also favoured the class argument claiming that differential access to socio-economic resources produces different life chances and that these "determine patterns of family living" (1990, p. 90).

One of the findings that remains unexplained in both Allen (1979) and Zinn and Eitzen's (1990) analyses is why, if class is the main explanatory factor, there are such marked differences between lower class whites and blacks in terms of their propensity to live in extended family households. As can be noted from the table below, extended family households were more than twice as common among low SES blacks than low SES whites in Allen's study.

In fact, even among whites with low income, low occupational status and low educational levels, nuclear families are clearly in the majority whereas this is not true of low SES blacks. Moreover, the proportion of nuclear families for low SES whites exceeds that of high SES blacks. It would seem then that factors other than mere economic need are responsible for these differences. While accepting this by pointing out that the impact of "family values" on domestic arrangements cannot be discounted, Allen's general conclusion is nevertheless on the side of socio-economic factors:

> Strong associations between family SES and family structure (family headship and composition) suggest significant class effects on family structure across races. Thus, non-conventional family structure is more common among lower than upper SES families; at the same time more Black families are concentrated at the lower SES levels. So clearly, economic deprivation must be a factor in the decisions of Black families to improvise and adopt alternatives to conventional family structure. Given the relationships observed in these data, it seems

reasonable to expect that class will be a better predictor of family structure than race.

Our conclusions notwithstanding, questions surrounding the relative effects of class and culture on Black family life in the urban United States remain largely unresolved (Allen, 1979, p. 310).

Table 4.1 Household Structure, Race and Socio-Economic Status, in the United States, in percentage

Household Structure	High SES	Low SES	High SES	Low SES
Husband/Wife Nuclear	87	75	73	49
Husband/Wife Extended	7	5	10	11
Female Head Nuclear	3	14	10	26
Female Head Extended	3	6	7	14
Total:	100	100	100	100

Source: Allen, 1979:309.[1]

Similarly mixed findings have emerged from more recent attempts to test these explanations for race differences in family patterns in the United States. Tienda and Angel (1982), for example, also found that even after adjustments were made for differences in socio-economic factors, black households were 12% more likely to be extended than white households (1982, p. 521). Contrary to Allen, they found that education is negatively related to household extension. Each year of schooling reducing the likelihood of extended family households by 2% (1982, p. 521). The greater tendency for households headed by never married female heads to be extended also forms an important part of their analysis and, like Allen, they hypothesise that it is because black families are more likely to be headed by never married women that they are also more likely to be extended. Their analysis also showed that among female headed households, education is positively related to extendedness. They claim that among low educated female heads, welfare and other forms of public assistance act as a substitute for kin thereby reducing the likelihood of living with others in order to overcome economic difficulties. They draw the following conclusion:

On balance, the results provide some support for both the economic and the cultural explanations of the formation of extended households. It is impossible to choose unequivocally between these two explanations. The fact that female headship and education exert consistently significant effects, although in opposite directions, on the three measures of family extension[2] is perhaps the strongest evidence for the indeterminacy of the relative importance of the cultural versus the economic argument of extended household structure ... While it might seem appropriate to infer that cultural norms in favour of extended family living arrangements do operate to condition the differences in the composition of minority and non-minority families, our sense is that this conclusion would be premature, except on a tentative basis (Tienda and Angel,1982, p. 526-528).

Another contributor to this debate has been McAdoo, who has shown that even upwardly mobile blacks maintain strong extended family ties. This she explains both with reference to racial discrimination and culture. Zinn and Eitzen summarise McAdoo's argument as follows:

... socially mobile Blacks draw upon their families for more than financial aid. They depend on their families for strong emotional and cultural support as well ... the extended family pattern has developed into a strong and valuable cultural pattern because even for more secure Blacks, wider community support is always problematic. Racism has often necessitated the use of internal family resources that may not need to be tapped in by other families in society (McAdoo,1978 cited in Zinn and Eitzen,1990, p. 122).

McAdoo's analysis points to some of the factors that complicate this debate when applied to a comparison of black and white household structures. These are: racial oppression and the close association between class and ethnicity/race. The significance of the former is that by exacerbating the impact of social class on family patterns. It means that the position of lower class whites and blacks are not directly comparable. As McAdoo indicates, racial oppression may be an additionally significant variable accounting for the greater propensity towards extended family arrangements among blacks than whites (McAdoo in Zinn and Eitzen,1990). Second, the fact that blacks are far better represented in the lower than upper socio-economic categories means that the same group which is purported to ascribe to values which favour extended family arrangements is also more likely to be poor, thus making it difficult to ascertain the effect of class and culture.

A third complicating factor has been the inadequate way in which the notion of culture has been addressed. In none of the analyses referred to above does one find any description of Black/African or African American culture. Rather, Allen (1979) as well as Tienda and Angel (1982) treat culture as a residual category which is presumed to have an effect if class cannot be shown to have a statistically significant relationship to household structure.

It was in an effort to avoid these complicating factors while asking the same question about class, culture and household structure, that it was decided to focus on a community which is divided on the basis of ethnicity but where the ethnic groups are similar in terms of socio-economic status and racial oppression is not at issue. The ethnic categories in question are English and Afrikaans-speaking white South Africans. Given their longer exposure to rural living, strong attachment to the church and their more conservative political and moral ideas (Peele and Morse, 1974), it was hypothesised that Afrikaans speakers would ascribe to family values which favour extended family arrangements to a greater extent than English speakers. Moreover, although historically, Afrikaans speakers have been more heavily concentrated in the lower socio-economic categories than English speakers (Peele and Morse, 1974), it has been argued that decades of Afrikaner rule have resulted in a substantial erosion of the class dimension to the English-Afrikaans divide (Butler, 1975). Finally, the community which forms the empirical basis of this analysis is one in which the group which is believed to have a culture which favours extended family arrangements, dominated politically at the time.

Survey of Whites in Grahamstown

The models presented later derive from the findings of a survey which took place in 1991 involving 300 white households in Grahamstown, a small city located in the Eastern Cape Province of South Africa. Two residential areas which contrast in terms of socio-economic status (as measured by property prices) were identified for the study and 125 households in each of these areas were selected. A third area consisting of blocks of flats was also included (50 households).[3] The sampled population constitutes about 10% of all white households in Grahamstown. Both occupational status and residential area were taken as indicators of social class while ethnicity was identified by means of the respondent's mother tongue. The main question that guided the empirical research was: Can any observed variations in household patterns be explained with reference (a) to the respondent's mother tongue and\or (b) her class position? The concept of household structure was operationalised by distinguishing between those instances where the respondent lived alone (single person household); with a spouse only (couple household); with a spouse and children (nuclear family household); with her children but not a spouse (single parent household) with relatives other than a spouse or children (extended family households).

Regarding this item, the survey results show the statistical predominance of the nuclear family and the phases in the domestic life cycle associated with it (single person and couple households). Indeed, these three household structures accounted for 85% of all households and 80% of the population covered by the survey. Conversely, the results show that in the community in question, extended family households are extremely rare. That Grahamstown residents are by no means unique with respect to these findings is revealed by a comparison of the results of a nation-wide survey and the Grahamstown study (see Table 4.2). The only noticeable difference here is the higher proportion of nuclear family and lower proportion of couple households in Grahamstown, a finding that is in all probability related to the fact that the relatively large number of schools in the city makes it attractive for young couples with children.

Cross-tabulation of household structure and respondent's mother tongue revealed no statistically significant relationship ($p > 0.05$) (Table 4.3). Extended families were nevertheless more common among Afrikaans speakers than English speakers. The same was not, however, true of the relationship between household structure and class (Table 4.4).

While the small number of extended family households limits the value one can place on the information pertaining to them, the data revealed an inverse relationship between occupational status and family extension. This was also the case when area of residence was considered (see Table 4.5). It is furthermore noteworthy that Steyn's nation-wide survey involved a much larger number of extended family households in absolute terms (112 of a total of 1,746) and revealed the same pattern with respect to social class and family extension that was found in the Grahamstown study (1993, p. 50). Steyn did not consider home language.[4]

Table 4.2 Grahamstown Sample Compared to National Sample of White South Africans, in percentage

Household Structure	Whites in Grahamstown (1991)	White South Africans (1988 and 1989)
Nuclear	51	46
Couple	17	24
Single Person	17	15
Extended	4	6
Single Parent	5	5
Other	7	4
TOTAL:*	100	100

Source: Steyn, 1993, p. 39.
*Totals may not add to 100% due to rounding.

Table 4.3 Household Structure by Mother Tongue, in Grahamstown, in percentage

Household Structure	English	Afrikaans	Total
Single Parent	4	7	5
Nuclear	51	52	51
Couple	17	21	18
Single Person	19	11	16
Extended	3	4	3
Other	7	5	7
Total:	101	100	100

$\xi^2 = 4.72$, df $= 5$, p $= 45$

An unanticipated and significant finding to emerge from the study was that the two main independent variables (class and culture) were themselves found to be related (p < .004). Specifically, the results show that English speakers were more often represented in the professional category than Afrikaans speakers (50% vs. 28%) and that the opposite is true of the manual category (31% vs.

48%), see Table 4.6.

Table 4.4 Household Structure by Occupation, in Grahamstown, in percentage

Household Structure	Professional	Middle	Manual	Total
Single Parent	3	10	3	4
Nuclear	63	46	53	56
Couple	11	25	25	19
Single Person	19	12	9	14
Extended	1	3	4	3
Other	4	3	6	4
Total:	101	99	100	100

$\xi^2 = 21.51$, df = 10, p = .02

Table 4.5 Household Structure by Area, in percentage

Household Structure	Area I (Upper)	Area II (Lower)	Area III (Flats)
Single Parent	2	7	4
Nuclear	74	44	13
Couple	14	22	21
Extended	2	5	0
Single Person	6	15	50
Other	2	8	13
Total:	100	101	101

$\xi^2 = 82.76$, df = 10, p < .001

Table 4.6 Language by Occupational Category, in percentage

Occupation	English	Afrikaans
Professional	50	28
Middle	19	24
Manual	31	48
Total:	100	100

$\chi^2 = 11.32$, df = 2, p< .004

Language was also shown to be related to area of residence: A larger proportion of Afrikaans speakers residing in the lower than upper areas and the converse being true of English speakers (table not provided).

Given this finding, as well as the fact that age was also found to be related to household structure, Table 4.7 shows the results of a multivariate analysis involving these factors. In the presentation, age has been kept constant by only focussing on the 31-50 age category. Furthermore, only the two extreme occupational categories have been used.

These data suggest that Afrikaans speakers in the manual occupations differ from all of the other categories in terms of their propensity to live in particular kinds of household structures. Indeed, whereas nuclear families account for the vast majority of all of the other categories including English speakers in the manual occupational category (82%), they constitute less than 60% of lower class Afrikaans households.[5] Moreover, if one adds nuclear families, couple households and single person households one notices that 90% of professional English speakers, all of the manual English speakers and 94% of professional Afrikaans speakers live in such households, while the comparable figure for lower class Afrikaans speakers is only 76%. Since class seems to make a difference only within the Afrikaans category, this suggests that culture cannot be discounted in explanations for variations in household structures. Indeed, responses to one of the questions directed towards ascertaining the family values of respondents revealed that Afrikaans speakers (but not lower class respondents generally) were more positively inclined towards extended family arrangements than others. Working with the expectation derived from other studies (Clark, 1978; van der Merwe in Simkins, 1986) that the vast majority of white respondents would disapprove of living with their parents after marriage or attaining adulthood, respondents were asked whether they thought it unhealthy for married children to live very close to their parents. In other words, the question enquired about living *near* kin rather than *with* kin. The results here revealed that while only 39% of Afrikaans speakers responded affirmatively to this question, this applied to nearly half (47%) of English speakers (Table 4.8). Furthermore, it is noteworthy that nearly one quarter of Afrikaans speakers gave a conditional response (depends category), which suggests some degree of experience of extended family arrangements or having had to deal with the possibility thereof.

Table 4.7 Household Structure by Language and Occupation in 31-50 Age Category, in percentage

Household Structure

	Professional	*Manual*	*Professional*	*Manual*
Single Parent	6	0	0	12
Nuclear	80	82	75	59
Couple	4	18	13	18
Extended	2	0	6	12
Single Person	6	0	6	0
Other	2	0	0	0
Total:	100	100	100	101

Comparisons with Blacks in Grahamstown

Before considering some of the theoretical lessons that can be learned from these findings, the results of the survey of white Grahamstonians are compared to two recent studies of households located in the black residential areas of the city. The studies in question are those of Manona (1988) and Brown (1996).

The most striking finding to emerge from this comparison is that whereas the extended family clearly constitutes the mode in the case of black residents, this position is held by the nuclear family in the case of white residents (58% and 63% compared with 51% respectively). What is also evident is the very low proportion of couple and single person households in the two black samples, phases in the domestic life cycle associated with the nuclear family pattern

Table 4.8 Views on Neo-local Residential Setting by Language, in percentage

Unhealthy	English	Afrikaans	Total
Yes	47	39	32
No	43	38	46
Depends	10	23	23
Total:	100	100	101

$\xi^2 = 8.31$, df = 2, p< .02

Table 4.9 Comparison of Household Structures of Black and White Residents of Grahamstown, in percentage

Household Type		White Residents	
	Manona	*Brown*	*Ziehl*
	1988	1996	1991
Nuclear	18	17	51
Couple	5	1	17
Single Person	4	2	17
Extended	58	63	4
Single Parent	10	13	5
Other	5	4	7
Total:*	100	100	100

*Totals may not add to 100% due to rounding.

(Table 4.9). Also of note is the very low percentage of extended family households in the case of whites. Indeed the data show that 76% of the households in Manona's study and 80% of Brown's sample represent one of the phases of the domestic life cycle associated with the extended family pattern (nuclear plus extended family households), while 85% of the white households are in one of the phases of the domestic life cycle associated with the nuclear family (single person, couple and nuclear family households). Commenting on the results of his study, Manona writes:

> The most common type of household is one which is **based** on the nuclear family. However, the members of a household are rarely restricted to the husband, wife and children and it is also unusual for people to live either alone or only with their spouses, (Manona, 1988, p. 393, emphasis added).

He furthermore explains the high incidence of extended (or multiple family households) among blacks in Grahamstown by claiming that unemployment, illness, natural disasters and personal crises are such that "the household *must* assume responsibility for the welfare of the wider kinship group" (Manona, 1988, p. 393, emphasis added). This apparent class explanation is supported by the clear differences in socio-economic status between white and black Grahamstonians.[6] While the latter point hardly needs support, presenting a simple class argument without taking account of differences in cultural disposition brings us back to the question that was asked at the outset of this study: What is the role of class and/or culture in explaining variation in household structure between different communities?

Towards a Theoretical Model

The comparison of black and white households in Grahamstown and nation-wide (see Steyn, 1993) largely confirms Allen's finding with respect to the United States, namely that there are distinct race-differences in the propensity to live in extended family households (Allen,1979). Allen also found that class was related to household structure, with conventional family structures being more common in the upper than lower socio-economic categories. But contrary to the South African data, Allen did not find that extended families *per se* were more common in the lower than upper socio-economic categories (1979). I submit that this has something to do with the population structure of the United States, as whites are clearly in the majority and that within this culture, extended family households are extremely rare, even in the lower socio-economic categories. Indeed, Allen found that lower class whites have more in common with upper than lower class blacks as far as the tendency to live in conventional family structures is concerned. Below I present a model of the relationship between class, culture and household structure derived from the Grahamstown survey that may elucidate this finding.

If class was the only or even the major variable in explaining variations in lower class English and Afrikaans speakers to exhibit similar household patterns. In particular, one would have expected both groups to have an above average propensity to live in extended family households.

Poor Material Conditions —————→ Extended Family Households

Good Material Conditions ————→ Nuclear Family Households

This was not found to be the case since lower class Afrikaans speakers were far less likely than lower class English speakers to live in nuclear family households and more likely to live in extended family households. As noted, the same is true of Allen's study when lower class whites are compared to lower class blacks: 75% vs 49% in the case of nuclear family households and 11% vs 25% in the case of extended family households.

On the other hand, if culture was the overriding variable, one would have expected Afrikaans speakers to be significantly more likely than English speakers to reside in extended family and less likely to reside in nuclear family households regardless of socio-economic factors.

English Speakers —————→ Nuclear Family Households

Afrikaans Speakers —————→ Extended Family Households

Again, this was not found to be the case when considering nuclear family households since in both groups these constituted about half of all households. Moreover, multivariate analysis revealed that upper class Afrikaans speakers have more in common with both lower and upper class English speakers than with lower class Afrikaans speakers as far as nuclear family arrangements are concerned. 59% of manual Afrikaans households were nuclear, compared to over 75% of all the other groups. Regarding extended families, Afrikaans speakers were found to be more likely than English speakers to live in such households (4% vs. 3%) though this was not statistically significant. Moreover, multivariate analysis revealed that it was lower class Afrikaans speakers who were primarily responsible for these differences (12% of manual Afrikaans households vs. 6% of professional Afrikaans households). There were therefore distinct differences between lower and upper class Afrikaans speakers that did not apply in the same degree to English speakers.

In Allen's study the equivalent expectation would have been that lower and upper class blacks are similar in terms of their propensity to reside in extended family households. Allen's data showed that this is not the case when both female- and couple- headed extended family households are considered (25% low SES vs 17% high SES). Moreover, in line with the results of the Grahamstown study, Allen's data show that in the case of nuclear family living there are distinct differences between lower and upper class blacks and that this does not apply to whites. Both studies therefore show that it is only within a particular community that class appears to impact on household structure.

These findings bring us to the conclusion that class and culture combine in a particular way to produce different propensities to live in different types of households. The clue to understanding the nature of this combination in the Grahamstown study is provided by lower class Afrikaans speakers, who, as mentioned, distinguish themselves from all the other groups by having a greater propensity to live in extended family arrangements. Multivariate analysis involving age, language, occupation and views on extended family arrangements furthermore revealed that this group was also less inclined than their professional counterparts and English speakers generally, to regard such arrangements as unhealthy (Table 4.10). In the presentation, age has been kept constant

Table 4.10 Views on Neo-Local Residential Setting by Language and Occupation in the 31-40 Age Category, in percentage

Is living very close to parents after marriage unhealthy ?	English		Afrikaans	
	Professional	*Manual*	*Professional*	*Manual*
Yes	41	52	46	29
No	49	33	31	53
Depends	10	14	23	17
Total:	100	99	100	99

by only focusing on the 31- 40 age category. The following general statements have been deduced from the findings:

1. Extended family households are unlikely when the culture of the group proscribes them and material conditions do not necessitate them (professional English speakers) (Upper class whites).

2. Extended family households are also unlikely to occur when the culture of the group does not proscribe them but material conditions do not necessitate them (professional Afrikaans speakers) (Upper class blacks).

3. Extended family households are only likely to occur in significant numbers in those instances where a culture which positively evaluates them combines with low socio-economic status (Manual Afrikaans speakers) (Lower class blacks).

The model below summarises these observations:

Cultural Group favours:	Material Conditions	Household Structure
Nuclear Families	Good	Nuclear
Nuclear Families	Poor	Nuclear
Extended Families	Good	Nuclear
Extended Families	Poor	Extended

Figure 4.1 Model of Relationship among Material Conditions, Culture and Household Structure (I)

In terms of this model then, poor material conditions represent a necessary but not sufficient condition for an above average propensity to live in extended family households. Here, lower class English speakers (and lower-class whites generally) are an example of a group whose material conditions favour extended family arrangements but whose culture proscribes them.

This finding suggests that culture is the dominant variable since class only comes into play in those instances where its direction of influence (poor material conditions favouring extended family households) is the same as that which the culture defines as desirable. Such a conclusion would, however, be premature since the notion of culture needs further analysis and more needs to be said about the relationship between class and culture.

Relationship between Class and Culture

Above I have used the phrase the "culture of the group" deliberately in order to differentiate it from the culture to which the individual ascribes or aspires. It is of course possible that individuals who, on the basis of an objective criterion such as mother tongue are assigned to a particular cultural or ethnic group, aspire to a set of cultural ideals and practices associated with another group. This is likely to occur in those instances where the individual's cultural group (objectively defined) is not the dominant one.

Under such circumstances, upward mobility may involve not only an improvement in life chances but also acculturisation, i.e., the acceptance of the culture of another group. In those instances where the dominant group proscribes extended family arrangements (and favours nuclear ones) while the cultural group to which the individual belongs in an objective sense does not, nuclear families are likely to predominate (a) because material conditions permit them and (b) because the individual identifies with the values and norms of the dominant group. I submit that this is the case with respect to upper class or professional Afrikaans speakers for whom English speakers represent a reference group. Even though Afrikaans speakers have dominated politically from the 1940's to the 1990's, it is likely that because of their economic dominance, it has been the life-style of English speakers that has served as the aspirational ideal for Afrikaans speakers capable of emulating the behavioural patterns which make up that life-style.

On the basis of these observations, the proposed model is revised in the manner of Figure 4.2.

Cultural Group favours:	Material Conditions	Identify with dominant culture	Household Structure
Nuclear Families	Good	Yes	Nuclear
Nuclear Families	Poor	Yes	Nuclear
Extended Families	Good	Yes	Nuclear
Extended Families	Poor	No	Extended

Figure 4.2   Model of Relationship among Material Conditions, Culture and Household Structure (II)

From a processual point of view one can present this interpretation as follows:

Example I: Upper class Afrikaans speakers.

1. Objective culture does not proscribe extended family arrangements.
2. Material conditions are good.
3. Subjective identification with another culture which does proscribe extended family arrangements.
4. Low prevalence of extended family arrangements.

Example II: Lower class Afrikaans speakers.

1. Objective culture does not proscribe extended family arrangements.
2. Material conditions are poor.
3. Subjective identification with native culture (the culture of the group to which the individual has been objectively assigned).
4. Relatively high prevalence of extended family arrangements.

This analysis suggests that lower class English speakers are the exception in that they are the only group where the impact of material conditions is not reinforced by the impact of culture. As noted, social class is a necessary but not sufficient condition for the prevalence of extended family households, its impact being mediated by the cultural disposition of the individuals concerned.

Applying this model to a comparison of black and white household structures, lower class whites would be in a similar position to lower class English speakers in that material conditions may favour extended family households but their culture proscribes them. Upper class blacks would be in the opposite position if it is assumed that there is cultural homogeneity within the black community. On the other hand, if upper class blacks ascribe to Western family values then they would be in a situation similar to upper class Afrikaans speakers: Material conditions do not necessitate extended family arrangements and the culture with which they identify does not favour them. Finally, it is only among lower class blacks that one is likely to find both a relatively high incidence of extended family arrangements and family values consonant with that reality.

A survey among first year sociology students at Rhodes University in 1994 provides some support for the ideas expressed above. In the study respondents were asked to list the people with whom they lived at the age of 15. They were also asked whether they feel there is any obligation on the part of their parents to take in a relative in need of accommodation. The results show that black students were more likely than others to have lived in extended family arrangements and to respond affirmatively to the second question (Tables 4.11 and 4.12).[7]

Table 4.11   Students' Domestic Situation at Age 15

Household Structure	Black Students		Other Students		Total	
	N	%	N	%	N	%
Nuclear	22	46	80	84	102	71
Extended	12	25	5	5	17	12
Single Parent	9	19	7	7	16	11
Other	5	10	3	3	8	6
Total	48	100	95	99	143	100

Totals may not add to 100 due to rounding.

Black students were differentiated from other students on the basis of home language.

Table 4.12   Views on Whether Parents are Obliged to Take in a Relative in Need

Answer	Black Students		Other Students		Total	
	N	%	N	%	N	%
Yes	34	72	55	59	89	64
No	13	28	38	41	51	36
Total	47	100	93	100	140	100

Question: If a relative (such as an aunt, cousin or grandparent) is unemployed and cannot afford to pay for accommodation, do you think there is an obligation on the part of your parents to take them in?

Moreover, when the type of school from which the student had matriculated was taken into account, it was found that black students who had attended private schools were less likely than others to feel that their parents are obliged to take in a relative in need of accommodation (Table not provided). In particular, whereas about half of the black students who had matriculated from a private school responded affirmatively to that question, this applied to about 80% of the other black students. Therefore, while students cannot be seen as representative of the wider society, there is at least the suggestion here that the above model may well apply in the South African context when blacks and whites are compared.

Conclusion

The purpose of this chapter has been to consider the question of explaining variation in household structure in a setting where the group which is purported to favour extended family arrangements is not subject to racial discrimination or of a lower socio-economic status than the group to which it is being compared. While the latter assumption proved to be unfounded and the population as a whole showed a very low propensity for extended family living, the study of English and Afrikaans speaking white South Africans produced data which suggest a particular model of the relationship among class, culture and household structure. A crucial aspect of this model is that class and culture should not be treated independently of one another, i.e., as alternative explanations for the prevalence of specific household structures as has hitherto been the case. Rather, in terms of the proposed model, the community is seen as divided along both class and ethnic lines and depending on which ethnic group dominates economically as well as the particular family structure(s) favoured by this group, different propensities to reside in different household arrangements will arise.

Notes

1   Data reworked for presentation. Only households where the head has either high or low scores on all three measures of socio-economic status have been included. Other permutations, example low income and high education have been omitted.

2   Measures of extension: (1) presence of one or more non-nuclear members of any age; (2) the presence of one or more adult non-nuclear members, and (3) the presence of one or more economically active non-nuclear members (Tienda and Angel, 1982, p. 518).

3   Since white Grahamstonians are known to be relatively wealthy, the sample was not selected randomly but rather deliberately skewed in order to ensure an adequate representation of lower class households. However, the weighting of responses on the basis of known characteristics such as the fact that less than 10% of whites were employed in manual occupations in 1991, showed that the results were not substantially different (Central Statistical Services: Report Number 03-01-08:282).

4   Taking educational achievement as an indicator of social class, Steyn found that with respect to male-headed households, extended families were present in 23.3% of cases where the man's highest educational achievement was matric (completed high school) or below, compared to 3.6% of cases where he had attained a higher educational level (1993: 50). In the case of female headed households, the respective percentages are 9.1% (matric and below) compared with 0.8% (above matric) (Steyn, 1993, p.50).

5   The comparable figures for **conventional** (i.e. first marriage) nuclear families is: 80.3% of "Professional" English speakers; 81.8% "Manual" English speakers; 75% "Professional" Afrikaans speakers and only 47.1% of "Manual" Afrikaans speakers (table not provided).

6   The per capita income of those included in Manona's study ranged from nothing to R150.00 per month, 74% having an income of between R20 and R80 per month (1988, p. 393) while the income of whites in the Eastern Cape and Border region is estimated to be about five times as high as those of blacks (Erwee and Radder in Black et al, 1986, p. 21).

7   Black students were also more likely to feel that such a sense of obligation exists even where the relative was not in need of accommodation but simply expressed a wish to reside with them (26% compared with 10%) (table not provided).

References

Allen, W. R. (1979), Class, Culture, and Family Organisation: The Effects of Class and Race on Family Structure in Urban America. *Journal of Comparative Family Studies*, 10:301-313.

Black, P.A., McCartan, P.J. and Clayton, P.M. (1986), *A Demographic and Socio-Economic Profile of Region D.* Development Studies Working Paper No.30. Institute of Social and Economic Research, Rhodes University, Grahamstown.

Brown, B. (1996), *Where are the Men? An investigation into Female-Headed Households in Rini, with Reference to Household Structures, the Dynamics of Gender, and Strategies against Poverty.* M.A. Thesis. Grahamstown: Rhodes University.

Butler, J. (1975), The Significance of Recent Changes within the White Ruling Caste. In Thompson, L. and Butler, J. (eds). *Change in Contemporary South Africa.* Berkeley: University of California Press, pp. 79-103.

Kellerman, A.P.R. (1987), Expectations of and Commitment to Marriage. In Steyn et al. (eds). *Marriage and family life in South Africa: Research Priorities.* Pretoria: HSRC, pp. 531-565.

Manona, C. (1988), *The Drift from Farms to Town.* Ph.d Thesis, Grahamstown: Rhodes University.

Parsons, T. (1954), *Essays in Sociological Theory.* Glencoe: The Free Press.

Parsons, R. (1956), The American Family: Its Relations to Personality and the Social Structure. In Parsons, T. & Bales, R. (eds). *Family, Socialisation and Interaction.* New York: The Free Press, pp.3-33.

Peele, S. and Morse, S. (1974), Ethnic Voting and Political Change in South Africa. *The American Political Science Review,* 68:1520-1541.

Simkins, C. (1986), Household Composition and Structure in South Africa. In Burman, S. & Reynolds, P (eds). *Growing up in a Divided Society.* Johannesburg: Ravan Press, pp.16-42.

Steyn, A. (1993), *Gesinstrukture in die RSA* Report HG/MF-4. Research Programme on Marriage and Family Life. Pretoria: HSRC.

Tienda, M. and Angel, R. (1982), Headship and Household Composition Among Blacks, Hispanics, and Other Whites. *Social Forces,* 61(2):508-531.

Zinn, M.B. and Eitzen, S.D. (1990), *Diversity in Families.* New York: Harper Collins.

5 Cultural Adaptation and Change: Aboriginal Peoples in Manitoba Maintain their Differences

RACHEL LAWRENCHUK AND CAROL D. H. HARVEY

Introduction

A growing number of Aboriginal peoples across Canada are involved in revitalising their cultures while maintaining their differences. Many of the changes in Aboriginal culture originate at home; other changes are initiated in courts, in schools and by collective action. In this chapter we examine Aboriginal cultural history in Canada, particularly as it relates to family daily life and to education. We then examine literature on current cultural change, with a specific focus on the Canadian province of Manitoba. This literature is illustrated with examples from research on Manitoba Aboriginal women by the authors (Eni Lawrenchuk, 1988; Lawrenchuk and Harvey, 2000; Lawrenchuk, Harvey, and Berkowitz, 2000) and personal communication with two Manitoba Aboriginal men.

Any culture is under continual change and adaptation in order to survive. The term culture denotes language, traditions, and material creations of people, as well as tensions of different opinions, struggle among competing persons within and outside it, and dynamic change (Dirks, Eley and Ortner, 1994; Haig-Brown, 1995). A culture is socially constructed in the day to day interaction among individuals. The measure and validity of a culture are determined by its efficacy as a design for living.

Aboriginal peoples in Canada are involved in keeping their cultures relevant and useful within the dominant culture while retaining core values. These efforts include the adaptation of traditional philosophies, principles, social and normative systems by embracing the rich diversity of knowledge and language through strong families, relevant education, and social action. Such processes are difficult, given the long history of colonisation of Aboriginals.

In this chapter we outline Canadian policies and practices directed toward Aboriginal peoples and their effects on Aboriginal individual and cultural self-determination. We focus on the history of intrusion by the Canadian government into Aboriginal families and education, followed by an examination of growing movement toward self-determination, including Aboriginal control of Aboriginal education, development of strong families, and social action. We describe examples of cultural change and adaptation which are gaining strength despite powerful external forces and conditions of domination.

More than 600,000 Canadian people, including status, non-status Indian, Métis and Inuit reported Aboriginal identity in 1991 (Statistics Canada, 1991); by the 1996 Census, there were 799,010 people of Aboriginal descent in Canada, 2.8% of the population (Statistics Canada, on-line). Indigenous peoples in Canada reside in distinct cultural areas, including northern communities, reserves and cities from Labrador on the east coast to Vancouver Island on the west. Presently there are at least 23 different Indigenous languages spoken in Canada (Statistics Canada, 1991). The Province of Manitoba, in which we did our research, is located in the east-west geographic centre of Canada, and had 128,685 Aboriginals in 1996 (12% of the population), and the City of Winnipeg had 45,750, which was 7% of its population (Statistics Canada, on line). It is estimated that Manitoba schools will have one-fourth of their student populations of Aboriginal descent in 10 years.

In order to understand the current cultural adaptation and change, knowledge of Canada's past practices toward Aboriginal peoples, particularly in the field of education, is necessary. A short history of colonisation by outsiders and within Canada is a place to begin.

Colonisation and Internal Colonisation

Aboriginal cultural adaptation and change occur in the context of institutional arrangements that were established earlier by the Europeans and later by the Canadian government.

The Europeans arrived in Canada after thousands of years of Aboriginal settlement. The British in North America incorporated Aboriginal peoples and cultures into a liberal economy and transferred their resources for the benefit of the colonisers (Davis and Zannis, 1973). The process of subjection of the

Aboriginal peoples was conducted in much the same way in Canada as it had been in other colonised areas of Africa, Asia and Latin America, by white European powers during the age of imperialism (Perley, 1992).

Later, the Canadian government took over where the British left off, using a process of internal colonisation, a term used to explain inequality and dependency within a country. Factors in an internal colonial relationship, such as in Canada, include (a) displacement of Aboriginal peoples by European expansion; (b) isolation and containment of Aboriginal peoples in a reserve system; (c) forced assimilation; (d) increasing political and economic domination of reserve affairs; and (e) the development of a racist ideology which portrays Aboriginal people as uncivilised, savage or childlike (Perley, 1992). Internal colonisation serves as an underlying framework for understanding the relationship between Aboriginal peoples and dominant Canadian society. For Aboriginal peoples, knowing this history can serve as a force which helps to "move beyond the personal dimension of (self-blame) and seek to heal the nation with each (individual's) small but determined steps" (Battiste, 1998, p. 24).

Assimilation and domination policies are meaningless and their power incomprehensible without an understanding of the concepts which drive them, the knowledge base which constitutes and defines them, empowers them, and justifies their existence and means of intervention (Hughes, 1995). The Euro-Canadian and later the Canadian government could not have imposed such intrusive policies onto a once independent, indigenous people without first forcing them into subjectivity and redefining them as problems in need of massive and intensive intervention (Hughes, 1995). This subjectivity was made possible through the intrusive political, social and economic practices of the colonisers, combined with their superior weapons and the spread of infectious diseases for which the Aboriginal peoples had not developed immunity (Hughes, 1995; Waldrum, Herring and Young, 1995; Young, 1988).

Power and Contradiction in Canadian "Indian" Policy

Much of the apparent contradiction in Canadian "Indian" policy derives from a Western liberal-humanist conscience. People in power recognised the rights and liberty of the Aboriginal peoples on the one hand, yet subscribed righteously to the duty of the state to "civilise" and "reform" them (Hughes, 1995) on the other. The message was that in protecting Aboriginal peoples administrators were to oversee their physical and cultural extinction; however, Aboriginal peoples survived despite comprehensive physical and cultural devastation (Hughes, 1995).

The Canadian government had to contend with Aboriginal resistance and the gaze of the outside world.   By 1960 Canada reacted to charges of mistreatment of Aboriginal peoples (Bartlett, 1988), but those efforts did not dissolve government intentions to assimilate Aboriginals into Canadian citizenship.

Over the past few decades Aboriginal, federal and provincial governments have engaged in negotiations concerning Aboriginal right to self-government. Although much effort is spent discussing self-determination issues, to date the concept remains undefined. For most Aboriginal leaders, self-government is the right to govern community cultural and political issues as per a people's organisational principles and philosophies.   It may mean a reordering of the Canadian confederation to make room for the inherent right of Indians to self-government (Boldt, 1993).

An interesting point is that the present form of colonisation, i.e., "self-government," represents a political paradox (Hughes, 1995).   Rather than encouraging governance by Aboriginals, the Canadian government is saying to Aboriginal nations, "be independent, go on and revive your cultures and political organisational frameworks, determine your destinies, under these (our) restrictive guidelines." Under this system, the elite Aboriginal peoples who are those most involved with self-governing activities, are also those employed by the federal, provincial governments or any of their institutions.   The elites become the most assimilated into and dependent upon the mainstream culture and politic (Hughes, 1995).

Before examining particular colonial practices and their effects on family life, it is useful to have a glimpse into traditional Aboriginal life. Information gained from Manitoba Aboriginal peoples is helpful to understand some traditions.

Traditional Family and Educational Life

Aboriginal peoples, despite differences in language and culture among them and colonisation imposed on them, did share several underlying and fundamental values, philosophies and principles. They taught their children these ideas, so that children would develop into healthy and successful adults. The common elements in Aboriginal education included the importance of the family and the community, the centrality of the child, respect for elders, a reliance on stories for teaching purposes and the use of ritualised ceremonies to impart rites-of-passage lessons (Castellano, 1986; Charter, 1996; Couture, 1987; Hart, 1996; Meili, 1991).

Roger Roulette, an Ojibway language and culture teacher and author, described the traditional Ojibway education he received as a child from village elders as follows:

> The elders would sit us down every day to teach us traditional values. These are the strength of a culture. They taught us who we are. They taught us the fundamental values of health, community and education. We were taught how to take care of ourselves, of our responsibility to ourselves and to others. We were taught of the importance of sharing and of respect. Without an understanding of these values you can't take pride in your culture or your language, nor can you understand the significance of who you are, of who your people are. The education would start at as early an age as possible and continue until puberty. It would be intensive. Sometimes our grandmother would wake us up at 4:30 in the morning to teach us our stories, our legends. I remember going out to the bush too. That's where we'd learn, from two weeks-- sometimes up to three months at a time—we'd be out there. Values, through stories, myths and legends. We'd learn philosophy, history and medicine, art and music. We would know who we are (R. Roulette, personal communication, September 15, 2000).

An educational system trains young people in the skills they require to become successful and productive members of their community (Miller, 1996). These skills include an ability to procreate and create, to preserve, provide and protect. Roger Roulette provides examples of the traditional education he received:

> The elders used to give us the training for independence. This training includes: 1). Cleanliness - this does not mean simply the lack of dirt, it is more. It is how to conduct yourself so that you do not make others sick. 2). Next, there is selective consumption - this means what is good for you to eat may not be good for me to eat, the way they used to push milk on lactose intolerant native children. For instance, federal guidelines for nutrition do not apply to us. A person must come to know through selective consumption what is beneficial to his/her health and what is not. 3). Now, the third principle is a good work ethic - we learned that it is important to be active, don't just lay around. To keep busy is to gain strength. 4). Finally, there is the principle of self-healing - first aid,

how to look after yourself. Basic first aid, everyone had to know (R. Roulette, personal communication, September 15, 2000).

According to Roger Roulette, the elders dedicated their lives to teach and to raise the children. "We are their legacy. They sacrificed their lives for us. In their honour we need always acknowledge them" (R. Roulette, personal communication, September 15, 2000).

Notwithstanding significant differences among the cultural groups, and therefore their systems of education, the various educational practices of the Aboriginal populations in Canada did share a common philosophical or spiritual orientation, as well as a similar approach (Miller, 1996). "For all these peoples, instruction was suffused with their deeply ingrained spirituality, an inevitable tendency to relate the material and personal in their lives to the spirits and the unseen. Moreover, they all emphasised an approach to instruction that relied on looking, listening and learning - the three Ls" (Miller, 1996, p. 16).

Addressing commonalties in the educational orientations of the original inhabitants of what is now Canada, cannot imply homogeneity among the groups. Roger Roulette tells us, "We are all distinct cultures. You would not go and lump together German and Russian history, so why would you consider lumping together Aboriginal cultures? It cannot be done" (R. Roulette, personal communication, September 15, 2000).

Internal Colonisation in Daily Life and in Education

The Indian Agent

Canadian practices which interfered with the private family and community lives of Aboriginal peoples included the positioning by the federal government of an "Indian agent," whose responsibilities included the management, surveillance and disciplining of Aboriginal peoples living on reserve lands. A former northern Manitoba Cree chief told us the agent was "in every sense, our lord and master. There wasn't a single facet of our lives that he didn't control" (M. Lawrenchuck, personal communication, September 10, 2000). In the Prairie Provinces, a "pass" system was established whereby the Indian Agent representing the federal government would control the movement of Aboriginal peoples. Aboriginals could not leave the reserve without a pass issued by the agent (Bartlett, 1988).

Residential Schools

Another extreme form of interference is the abduction of Aboriginal children and forced attendance at residential schools. Early attempts (1600s to 1700s) at Aboriginal education by the Catholic Church were deemed a failure (Miller, 1996). Parental resistance to separation from their children contributed to their failure, as well as the students' dislike to the confinement and regimentation that the schools demanded of them (Haig-Brown, 1988; Miller, 1996; Milloy, 1999).

Within 50 years of the establishment of British dominance in Canada, a segregated system of enforced schooling of Aboriginal children was put into place (Perley, 1992). Boarding, industrial and residential schools were established and run by religious groups who emphasised moral training and practical skills. The history of these schools in Canada can be learned from the works of Barman, Hebert, and McCaskill (1986); Chrisjohn (1998); Grant (1996); Haig-Brown (1988); Kelm (1998); Miller (1996); and Milloy (1999).

Education for Aboriginal peoples was planned and controlled by the Euro-Canadian government as early as 1847 (Barman, et al., 1986; Haig-Brown, 1988). The Canadian government made all of the educational decisions for Aboriginal children, in contrast to provincial control of education for the dominant society. These decisions included who would go to school, how long children would attend, what would be taught, and what language would be used (Perley, 1992). Under such an educational system the goals for Aboriginal populations served the needs of the Euro-Canadian government, not the Aboriginal peoples.

Many of the residential schools started in the 1880s and 1890s experienced problems in terms of attracting and retaining children (Miller, 1996). One reason for this is that Aboriginal families resisted the schools as organised attempts "to educate and colonise a people against their will" (Miller, 1996). Amendments to the Indian Act showed government frustration with trying to compel attendance at the schools.

By 1920, a clause was added to the Indian Act which made it mandatory for every child between the ages of seven and fifteen to attend school (Milloy, 1999). Further, the clause authorised "anyone appointed a truant officer to enter 'any place where he had reason to believe there are Indian children between the ages of seven and fifteen years to prescribe penalties for Indian parents who refused to comply with notice to make their children available for school'" (Miller, 1996, p. 169-70). With enforcement came resistance and even when penalties were greatest, Aboriginal parents and children still found ways to evade officials (Miller, 1996).

Of all of the forms of intrusion into private family and community cultural and political life, education was considered to be the principal agent of the assimilation policy (Miller, 1996; Milloy, 1999).   According to Deputy Superintendent Duncan Campbell Scott, who steered the administration of Indian Affairs from 1913 to 1932, education was "by far the most important of the many subdivisions of the most complicated Indian problem" (Milloy, 1999, p. 3). The most "potent power"" to influence cultural change was believed to be the education of children. This power was to be conducted through schools, and especially through residential schools (Milloy, 1999, p. 3).   Education would, according to Frank Oliver, the Minister of Indian Affairs (1908), "elevate the Indian from his condition of savagery" and make "him a self-supporting member of the State, and eventually a citizen in good standing" (Milloy, 1999, p. 3).

The residential school system was built on the premise that if Aboriginal communities were to "advance," it would occur only if the civilising system was amended to imbue Aboriginal people with the primary characteristics of civilisation, industry and knowledge (Milloy, 1999). In the schools, which were to be built off-reserves and away from white settlements, children would learn all manners of Western culture from religious education to style of dress and use of the English language (Barman, et al., 1986).

Boys would be provided training in husbandry, agriculture and mechanical trades; and girls would be trained in the domestic arts and sciences including dairying, needlework and cooking. ". . . by such instruction. . . the 'material and extensive change among the Indians of the rising generation (could) be hoping for'. In such schools, under the supervision of non-Aboriginal teachers and isolated from 'the influence of their parents,' pupils would 'imperceptibly acquire the manner, habits and customs of civilised life'" (Malloy, 1999, p. 13). The children were rarely engaged in the classroom or chapel. The amount of time they spent with books was small. Instead, the children were made to work long hours attending farming, maintenance, cooking and cleaning activities (Fournier and Crey, 1997; Miller, 1996).

The problem, then, was that the education provided to Aboriginal children by the church and government officials did not emanate from good will, but rather from a perceived obligation to convert the children from their paganism to Christianity and a need to stamp out any threat to the new Canadian regime. The assimilation through education was done by individuals who were not qualified teachers and who received meagre pay, if they received pay at all

(Miller, 1996; Milloy, 1999). The system was financed haphazardly by a government which continually searched for ways to cut costs. As the legal guardians of the Aboriginal children at the schools, they failed miserably in terms of the provision of education and basic needs.

Besides a poorly implemented curriculum by untrained and underpaid teachers, inefficiently constructed and run down buildings, disease epidemics and child slavery, the children were throughout the residential school experiment being subjected to all forms of physical, sexual and psychological abuses (Haig-Brown, 1988; Fournier and Crey, 1997; Miller, 1996; Milloy, 1999). These abuses would be acknowledged in reports to the government for decades without ever having the government recognise or intervene in these injustices, (being committed against *their* child wards), besides, perhaps, a slap to the wrist of the perpetrator (Miller, 1996).

Memories of Aboriginal peoples themselves of these schools are not so glamorous as the government had envisioned. One former pupil, a respondent in our research, told us

> I remember getting the strap. . . Every day we had straps for whatever reason. We weren't bad kids; we just had to be punished because of our colour. Or being made to stand with gum on our nose or to kneel. They didn't teach us anything real. I mean, how were we supposed to learn in that environment? I learned much later that most of those teachers weren't even certified (Lawrenchuk and Harvey, 2000, p. 88).

Aboriginal parents and community leaders resisted intrusion of the schools upon daily life. They deplored the purposeful denigration against their ways of life. They opposed having their children removed by force for eight to ten years. They contested the lack of relevant education their children had received. They felt their children were not being properly nourished and allowed to grow, and were in some cases maliciously attacked by incompetent teachers. The government archives are full of instances of parental and community resistance. All complaints, in spite of everything, would be met with deaf ears. Even when their children died, sometimes up to 75% of the student body, their complaints would merit little or no response (Fournier and Crey, 1997; Miller, 1996).

The Apprehension of Aboriginal Children

The child adoption practices which culminated in the massive removal of Aboriginal children in the 1960s could be said to have taken over where residential schooling left off (Castellano, 1986). The removal of Aboriginal children from their families meant their removal not only from their parents and immediate families, but also from their communities and cultural identities. The losses they would experience for the rest of their lives would be played out in sickness, depression, alcoholism, isolation, and shame. The effects of separation would be felt not only in the lives of those apprehended and by their parents and families, but in those of their children as well. This effect on the offspring of apprehended individuals may be psychological or physical, as in the case of fetal alcohol syndrome (Fournier and Crey, 1997; May, 1999).

The high rates of Aboriginal child apprehension, relative to the rates for whites, were made for three reasons. First, family health and child guidance were judged by social workers according to their own Eurocentric frameworks. In a study published in 1992, the researchers found that "Aboriginal children were taken away in hugely disproportionate numbers less for reasons of poverty, family dysfunction or rapid social change than to effect a continuation of the 'colonial agreement': that is: 'the child welfare system was part of a deliberate assault on Native society designed to make changes in Native people'" (Fournier and Crey, 1997, p. 84). The social worker, like the missionary, the priest and the Indian agent earlier, was convinced that the removal of Aboriginal children from their homes was the only salvation available to them (Fournier and Crey, 1997).

Second, consequences of Canadian policy which worked to destroy Aboriginal identities and independence was blamed on those individuals the policies set out to destroy in the first place. For instance, after four or five generations of residential school attendance Aboriginal people were expected to care for and educate their children. After one hundred years of parentless existence they were to be judged on their parenting skill. Failure to properly care for their children resulted in involuntary termination of parental rights (Castellano, 1986). Third, misguided federal policy left Aboriginal community life in states of emergency in regard to housing, sanitation, safe drinking water, and health and social services (Fournier and Crey, 1997). Under these harsh conditions families were doing the best they could, usually without the additional help of counselors, home service workers or childcare assistants.

As a result, adoption of Aboriginal children by people outside their communities continued for several decades. The following analogy by John Tootoosis of this legacy summarises the difficulties of Aboriginal peoples:

> When an Indian comes out of these places, it is like being put between two walls and left hanging in the middle. On one side are all the things he learned from his people and their way of life that was being wiped out, and on the other are the white man's ways which he could never fully understand since he never had the right amount of education and not be a part of it. There he is, hanging in the middle of the two cultures and he is not Indian. They washed away practically everything an Indian needed to help himself, to think the way a human person should in order to survive (Barman, et al., 1986, p. 10).

The Revitalisation of Aboriginal Cultures

Many members of Aboriginal cultural groups are presently active in reclaiming their traditions and making culture relevant and vital. This activity occurs in all areas from political culture to holistic health and education and develops in a variety of ways depending on the particular group.

Control of Education for School-age Children

One example of cultural revival for many Aboriginal groups is in education. Residential schools have been abandoned, and many Aboriginal communities now run their own educational systems. Band operated schools explicitly incorporate the policies advocated in the 1973 document, *Indian Control of Indian Education*, produced by the National Indian Brotherhood, namely parental responsibility and community control (Frideres, 1998). The number of band operated schools has increased from more than 100 in 1980 to 300 in 1990 with an average increase of 15 schools annually. Attendance at the schools continues to grow, from 2,842 children in 1976 to 34,674 in 1990, reflecting the attendance of more than 40 per cent of the total Aboriginal student body (Frideres, 1998).

A New Initiative: Preschool Education by Aboriginal Community

The Aboriginal Head Start Initiative incorporates the policies stated in the *Indian Control of Indian Education* document. Aboriginal Head Start is a national initiative funded by Health Canada. It is an early intervention strategy, which addresses the needs of young Aboriginal children living in urban centres, large Northern and Aboriginal communities. It is a comprehensive program designed to meet the spiritual, emotional, intellectual and physical needs of children and their parents. The Initiative employs locally controlled and administered Aboriginal non-profit organisations that consider parents to be the natural advocates of their children and families.

Aboriginal Head Start's mandate is to foster the overall development and education of children; support parents and guardians as the prime teachers and caregivers of their children; and ensure local community involvement in the planning, development, operation and evaluation of the program. The main components of each Aboriginal Head Start Program include the language and cultural education and academic preparation of children and their parents.

Parents told us that participation in the program was helpful to them both as parents and as individuals. In the voice of one program participant,

> I believed the program would help me and my children learn and get improved social skills. I believe the program helped me in many ways. The workshops helped me learn a lot about parenting and how to have a better relationship with my kids. . .I better understand my own life and my difficulties and I share my experiences and help other women. . ." (Lawrenchuk, Harvey, and Berkowitz, 2000, p. 27).

Another commented,

> The Head Start Program is a second home to me. The people are friendly and very easy to talk with. I learned a lot by participating in workshops about children and how they develop and learn and I learned about my grandsons. Being a traditional Indian woman, the cultural and language part of the program is also very important to me" (Lawrenchuk, Harvey, and Berkowitz, 2000, p. 29).

A third woman, a director of a Head Start program, recognised the importance of the program in building a sense of community and said,

In society today, everything is so compartmentalised. Different levels of government, for example, make decisions and these decisions may or may not have anything to do with the families living in our community. If we teach the parents the skills they need to empower themselves, they can carry these over to their children. The children grow; the family and even the extended family grows. The community will take care of itself. It's only through a community development process that our community will become stronger and it starts with the mothers here at our program (Eni Lawrenchuk, 1998, pp. 92-93).

Intertribal and Intercommunity Initiatives in Urban Areas

The numbers of Aboriginal peoples living in urban centres have increased dramatically over the past half-century. For urban Aboriginals to retain their Aboriginal identities the significant boundaries of Aboriginal nationhood must be cultural rather than race or territory (Boldt, 1993). Yet, most Aboriginal peoples living in urban centres identify themselves with a certain band/tribe and reserve (Boldt, 1993; Champagne, 1999).

To maintain Aboriginal identity in urban areas, Canadian Aboriginal peoples are establishing intertribal education centres, preventive health programs, community centres, university and college programs and cultural activities such as powwows. All of these have contributed to preserving band/tribal and Aboriginal identities among those who have become more or less separated physically from their communities/reserves (Champagne, 1999). Canadian multicultural policies can enhance these efforts.

It is also the case that urban Aboriginal peoples are participating in Canadian mainstream society and cannot escape becoming part of the Canadian class structure (Boldt, 1993). These developing structures cannot be transported back to the reserve/communal societies; rather, the reserves need to accommodate the successes of urban community members to prevent their becoming estranged from their people and their cultures (Boldt, 1993).

Reform of Child Welfare

Rather than advocating the forced removal of Aboriginal children from their homes when difficulties arise, attempts are being made to incorporate an Aboriginal perspective into child welfare. For example, in Manitoba reorganisation of Child and Family Services is being done to allow for more

Aboriginal control of third-party decisions made for Aboriginal parents and children (D. McDonnell, personal communication, September 28, 2000).

At the same time, more supports are available to assist child welfare workers. These include access to personal and addictions counselling, training for childcare, and access to health services.

Family Life Now and in the Future

Lives for most Aboriginal peoples in Canada include poverty, low educational attainment, and health problems, including high rates of diabetes and tuberculosis. Teen suicides, a source of family stress, are high, with the Aboriginal rates in Manitoba reported at ten times the rates for other groups (Sigurdson, Staley, Matas, Hildahl, and Squair, 1994). Families will need to have strength in order to overcome these difficulties. As appropriate services and programs are being developed, together with a trend of diminishing colonial practices, it is possible for more Aboriginal families to join the positive changes in cultural adaptation being made by some.

The Necessity of Language and Knowledge Revival

The revival of Aboriginal languages is a part of the process of cultural adaptation and change. In language are locked the past, with keys to the present and future. Language is a link to the ways of the ancestors, the Great Spirit and the natural and social world. In the words of our respondents,

> I always felt lost. I didn't even know I was an Indian. This lady used to call me her little apple, you know, red on the outside, white on the inside. I didn't even know what that meant. When I found out, I was mad. I started to want to find out about my identity. Well for me I think it's too late, so I want to concentrate on the kids, making sure they know (Lawrenchuk and Harvey, 2000, p. 89).

Another said,

> It's a deadly thought actually, that my mom would stop speaking Cree. She experienced too much pain and too much discrimination that she decided she wasn't going to put her kids through that. She wasn't going to teach us Cree (Eni Lawrenchuk, 1998, p. 105).

Aboriginal languages are now being taught in schools, to pre-schoolers in Head Start programs, to elementary and secondary school students, and to university and college students. In Manitoba, for example, Cree and Ojibway, the major Aboriginal languages are being offered at all educational levels. To date this language instruction is not yet available to all Aboriginal students, but efforts are being made to reach more of the target population each year.

Conclusion

After surviving two centuries of harsh intervention and domination at the hands of the British and Canadian governments, Aboriginal community members are emerging with new confidence and vision. Canadian preoccupation with assimilation has lost its vigour and a new relationship is being built based on respect for Aboriginal rights. The Supreme Court ratified the protection of these rights in the Canadian constitution in 1996 when Chief Justice Lamer declared:

> In the Aboriginal tradition, societal practices and customs are passed from one generation to the next by means of oral description and actual demonstration. As such, to ensure the continuity of Aboriginal customs and traditions, a substantive Aboriginal right will normally include the incidental right to teach such a practice, custom and tradition to a younger generation (Battiste, 1998, p. 16).

Implementing programs and services for cultural revitalisation is an essential and difficult task. The work requires of Aboriginal peoples that they use their own standards of evaluation and legitimisation, rather than those of the Euro-Canadian system.

In order to assess the impact of these political, educational, health and social initiatives on Aboriginal cultures, Aboriginal people will need to ask the following questions: Do the programs and services derive an Aboriginal world-view? Do they represent basic fundamental principles of the specific culture? Do they proceed according to the pace and direction of the community members? Are the programs controlled by people who hold Aboriginal interest paramount? In what ways are the programs and services dependent upon others? Are Aboriginal languages and knowledge embraced in every stage of development and implementation?

One mother expressed this idea as,

If we are going to have an Aboriginal education that is truly Aboriginal then it has to be controlled by Aboriginal people from the top levels, like an Aboriginal school division. They'd have to be dedicated to our children, to our language and culture, and have parents and families involved in every step of the education (Eni Lawrenchuk, 1998).

This chapter reviewed the history and described the resistance to domination and the activities of cultural adaptation and change of Aboriginal peoples. Substantial efforts are taking place across the country that are particular to certain communities, but others are national in scope and perspective. An example of the latter includes the National Aboriginal Head Start Initiative.

In the end, we are left with a question that requires further investigation. Do the programs and services outlined in the chapter indicate successes in the revitalisation of Aboriginal cultures?

Two requirements established by Perley, (1992) might provide food for thought:

1. *The pace and direction of development have to be determined by Aboriginal groups.* In essence, decolonisation is a process of liberation for both the colonised and the coloniser. It liberates the colonised from the shackles of control by an oppressive, dominating, and paternalistic society. Decolonisation also liberates the colonisers from their colonial mentality and preoccupation with control, superiority, and dominance over Aboriginal peoples. The fact that Aboriginal groups should determine the pace and direction of development should not be seen as a challenge to other Canadians.

2. *The process of decolonisation has to be driven and directed by the Aboriginal people.* The planning and decision-making processes regarding (program) change and initiatives are the responsibility of Aboriginal people. A decolonised education (or health prevention) system may have the effect of greater participation of Aboriginal people at all levels of a pluralistic system, but it is not a question of the "coloniser" opening up places to "accommodate" Aboriginals. Aboriginal people have the responsibility to decide the terms under which they participate; otherwise, relationships of dependency are reinforced.

References

Barman, J., Hebert, Y., and McCaskill, D. (1986). *Indian Education in Canada, Vol. 1: The Legacy.* Vancouver, BC: University of British Columbia Press.

Bartlett, R. H. (1988). Parallels in Aboriginal Land Policy in Canada and South Africa. *Canadian Native Law Reporter with Cumulative Indexes of Articles and Cases.* Saskatoon, Sask: University of Saskatchewan, Native Law Center.

Battiste, M. (1998). Enabling the Autumn Seed: Toward a Decolonized Approach to Aboriginal Knowledge, Language, and Education. *Canadian Journal of Native Education, 22(1),*

Boldt, M. (1993). *Surviving as Indians: The Challenge of Self-Government.* Toronto, ON: University of Toronto Press.

Castellano, M. B. (1986). Collective Wisdom: Participatory Research and Canada's Native People. *Convergence, 19(3),* pp.50-53.

Champagne, D. (1999). *Contemporary Native American Cultural Issues.* Walnut Creek, CA: AltaMira Press.

Charter, A. (1996). Integrating Traditional Aboriginal Teaching and Learning Approaches in Post-Secondary Settings in Jill Oakes and R. Riewe (eds), *Issues in the North, Volume 1,* (Pp.55-87). Winnipeg, MB: Canadian Circumpolar Institute.

Chrisjohn, R., and Young, S. (1998). *The Circle Game: Shadows and Substance in the Indian Residential School Experience in Canada.* Penticton, BC.: Theytus Books.

Couture, J.E. (1987). What is Fundamental to Native Education? Some Thoughts on the Relationship Between Thinking, Feeling and Learning in L. Stervin and S. McCann (eds), *Contemporary Educational Issues: The Canadian Mosaic.* Toronto, ON: Copp Clark Pitman, pp. 178-191.

Davis, R., and Zannis, M. (1973). *The Genocide Machine in Canada.* Montreal: Black Rose Books.

Dirks, N.B., Eley G., and Ortner, S.B. (1994). *Culture/Power/History: A Reader in Contemporary Social Theory.* Princeton, NJ: Princeton University Press.

Eni Lawrenchuk, R (1998). *Parent Participation in a Cree and Ojibway Head Start Program: Development of a Conceptual Framework.* University of Manitoba, Master's Thesis.

Fournier, S. and Crey, E. (1997). *Stolen From Our Embrace: The Abduction of First Nations Children and the Restoration of Aboriginal Communities.* Vancouver, BC: Douglas & McIntyre Ltd.

Frideres, J. (1998). *Aboriginal Peoples in Canada: Contemporary Conflicts, (5ᵗʰ ed.).* Scarborough, ON: Prentice Hall Canada.

Haig-Brown, C. (1988). *Resistence and Renewal: Surviving the Indian Residential School.* Vancouver: BC Tillacum Library.

Haig-Brown, C. (1995). *Taking Control: Power and Contradiction in First Nations Adult Education.* Vancouver, BC: University of British Columbia Press.

Hart, M. A. (1996). Sharing Circles: Utilizing Traditional Practice Methods for Teaching, Helping and Supporting in S. O'Meara and D. A. West (Eds.), *From Our Eyes: Learning From Indigenous Peoples.* Toronto, ON: Garamond Press, pp. 59-72.

Hughes, I. (1995). Dependent Autonomy: A New Phase of Internal Colonization. *Australian Journal of Social Issues, 29(2),* pp. 369-388.

Kelm, M. E. (1998). *Colonizing Bodies: Aboriginal Health and Healing in British Columbia 1900-50.* Vancouver, BC: UBC Press.

Lawrenchuk, R.. and Harvey. C. (2000). Parent Participation in a Cree and Ojibway Head Start Program in J. Oakes. R. Riewe. S. Koolage. L. Simpson, and N. Schuster (eds.) *Aboriginal Health, Identity and Resources.* Winnipeg, MB: University of Manitoba Departments of Native Studies and Zoology, and Faculty of Graduate Studies, pp. 83-92.

Lawrenchuk, R.. Harvey. C.. and Berkowitz, M. (2000). Parents and Children Together: The Development of the Oshki-majahitowiin Head Start Program. *Early Childhood Matters, June, pp.* 24-29.

May, P.A., (1999). The Epidemiology of Alcohol Abuse among American Indians: The Mythical and Real Properties in Duane Champagne (eds), *Contemporary Native American Cultural Issues.* Walnut Creek, CA: AltaMira Press. pp. 227-244.

Meili, D. (1991). *Those Who Know: Profiles of Alberta's Native Elders.* Edmonton, Alta: NeWest Press.

Miller, J. R. (1996). *Shingwauk's Vision: A History of Native Residential Schools.* Toronto, ON: University of Toronto Press.

Milloy, J. S. (1999). A *National Crime: The Government and the Residential School System, 1879-1986.* Winnipeg, MB: University of Manitoba Press.

Perley, D. G. (1992). Aboriginal Education in Canada as Internal Colonialism. *Canadian Journal of Native Education, 20(1),* pp. 118-128.

Sigurdson, E.. Staley, D.. Matas. M.. Hildahl, K., and Squair, K. (1994). A 5-year review of youth suicide in Manitoba. *Canadian Journal of Psychiatry, 39,* 397-403.

Statistics Canada (1991). *Aboriginal Peoples Survey: Language, Tradition, Health, Lifestyle and Social Issues.* Government of Canada.

Statistics Canada (2000). Population [OnLine], Available:www.statcan.ca/english/pgdb/ People/Population/demo39a.htm

Young, T. K. (1988). *Health Care and Cultural Change: The Indian Experience in the Central Subarctic.* Toronto: University of Toronto Press.

Waldram, J. B.. Herring. D.A.. and Young. T.K. (1995). *Aboriginal Health in Canada: Historical, Cultural and Epidemiological Perspectives.* Toronto: University of Toronto Press.

6 Conclusion

CAROL D. H. HARVEY

In this book we have seen a number of ways in which minority families are similar to the dominant culture or are apart from it. Factors that are important to maintaining differences by minority families are the cohesion of the local community, values taught by religion, and use of language. In addition race and social class are important affecting minority family functions. Finally social policy by the dominant society may either facilitate or hinder minority families. It is also the case that analysis of minority families may shed light on theories of family interaction and functioning, which often have been developed by researchers in the dominant culture. Analyzing the lessons of the research presented here is the purpose of this final chapter.

Importance of Community

In each of the five chapters in this book, people are said to live their daily lives within a community. When the community is strong and supportive, as in the case of the Old Order Mennonites in Canada, according to John Peters, families are helped to maintain their differences from the dominant culture. Likewise, conservative Christian communities reinforce beliefs about mothering young children which affect behaviour, including labour force participation of women, as Darren Sherkat has documented in the United States.

At times the community itself is undergoing change. Susan Ziehl shows the effect of social class and race on South Africans, particularly in their residential patterns. Rachel Lawrenchuk and Carol Harvey documented the effects of the dominant culture in Canada trying to change Aboriginal families to make them more like the dominant group, a process which challenged Aboriginal families but did not destroy them. Fatima Husain and Margaret O'Brien showed that Pakistani families in Britain have a great deal of within-group variation, but the evolution of community-based family life to a religious base has occurred over time.

Whether or not the community is supportive or undergoing change, it is very important for how families operate. From communities value orientations

89

arise, which in turn affect behaviour. Thus the Old Order Mennonite communities reinforce the beliefs of proper family behaviour, gender roles, development of skills in homemaking and farming, use of technology, and intergenerational transfer of wealth. Muslim values, somewhat different among various sects, reinforce gender roles and religious teachings. Cree and Ojibway families in Canada were challenged by the policies of the dominant culture which took children from them to be educated in residential schools, a process which denied traditional culture and values. Many of these families are now attempting to re-establish control over cultural life.

Role of Religion

In each of the chapters of this book authors show the central role of religion in family life. Darren Sherkat's research focuses on religion, demonstrating the effect of conservative Christian values on labour force participation of mothers of young children in the United States. Religious values set the Old Order Mennonites in Canada apart from their neighbours, and religion permeates all phases of daily life, according to the research of John Peters. Religion begins to assume a stronger, more important roles in defining the Pakistani families in Britain as community ties to particular locations in Pakistan weaken, according to the research of Husain and O'Brien. Although religion was not examined closely by Ziehl in Chapter 4, other South African research shows an effect of Calvinist religious values on Afrikaaner men (Smit, 2000). Finally, Aboriginal traditional religious values are assuming a place in the revitalisation of Cree and Ojibway families in Canada, according to Eni Lawrenchuk (1998) in the original research which forms a basis for Chapter 5.

Use of Language

Language is an important part of the intergenerational transmission of culture. When indigenous language use is discouraged or prohibited, as in the case of Cree and Ojibway children in the previous era of residential schools, cultural continuity is tested and at times broken. When people cannot speak the official language of a country, as in the case of some Pakistani women in Britain, access to social services and other advantages of the dominant society may be denied to families.

On the other hand language can serve as a social glue, reinforcing the distinctiveness of a cultural minority. Such is the case of speaking Pennsylvania Dutch among the Old Order Mennonites in Canada. Since many people can use English access to services, such as medical treatment, is available to these families.

Effects of Belonging to a Visible Minority

Having identifiable characteristics which set families apart from the dominant culture was reported here. These characteristics are often matters of race, where the minority family is different from the dominant society, even if the dominant group is in a statistical minority. Race is important for Pakistanis in Britain, for blacks in South Africa, and for Aboriginals in Canada, as we have seen.

Interestingly enough, the Old Order Mennonites belong to the dominant race in Canada, but they choose to be a visible minority by their distinctive dress and use of horses and buggies for transportation. In their case creating their visibility is a manifestation of the religious values they hold.

Social Class as an Important Predictor of Minority Family Behaviour

Susan Ziehl, in her chapter on race and class in South Africa, highlights the importance of social class in predicting family behaviour. Indeed, evidence she presents is persuasive in showing social class effects on families are stronger than race among her respondents. The poverty associated with being Aboriginal in Canada permeates family life, limiting choices for parents and children and creating dependence on social services. Greater reliance by Pakistanis than other British on social services is also related to social class among those families.

Social Policy of the Dominant Society

In all of the family groups discussed in this book, social policies of the dominant society have direct and sometimes very pervasive consequences on family functioning. The negative effect of past policies of the Canadian government on Aboriginal families is documented in the chapter by Lawrenchuk and Harvey.

Part of the cultural revitalisation and change among Aboriginal communities is directed toward overcoming problems created by governmental actions. The dramatic change of governmental apartheid policies in South Africa certainly influenced family life there.

The same Canadian government which created difficulties for Aboriginal families offered exemption from military service to Mennonites, which directly affected their decisions to immigrate into the country. This governmental policy assisted Mennonites in their ability to direct their own affairs and live according to religious values. Similarly, immigration policies in Britain had an effect on Pakistani family decisions to move from Pakistan to Britain.

Family Theory Applications

Family theory can be tested and/or modified by studying minority families. Generally family theory is generated by researchers from the dominant society, and application of that theory to minority families can show insight and bring modifications to the theory. In this book John Peters shows the relationship of theory to minority families most clearly in Chapter 1. The life cycle stage theories of Duvall and Hill do not clearly fit the Old Order Mennonites. Probably the same could be said of Aboriginal families in Canada or blacks in South Africa.

In contrast, family theory can mesh with value systems of the minority family quite well. For example, earlier work by Lawrenchuk and Harvey (2000) utilised human ecological theory. This theory interrelates concepts important to human ecology, including "the law, conditions, principles and ideals which are concerned on the one hand with [one's] immediate physical environment and on the other hand with [one's] nature as a social being and is the study specifically of the relationship between those two factors" (Bubolz and Sontag, 1993, p. 420). Aboriginal teachings of the medicine wheel, with its "interconnections among care giving responsibility, personal and cultural history and the search for meaning. . .parallel a human ecology perspective" (Lawrenchuk and Harvey, 2000, p. 91).

Summary

Readers of the research presented in this book are given a taste of the complexity of studying family life in racial or cultural minority families. Factors such as community strength, racial composition, use of language, and social class are important factors to consider in studying minority families.

The role of social policy is very important as well. If the dominant culture wants to facilitate family life, it can, via policies that encourage the development and nurture of healthy families. On the other hand social policies can discourage or even eliminate minority family functioning.

Researchers can test theory in the context of minority family behaviour and values. We can learn about family complexity and can enhance our understanding of family life through research. Insight can be obtained, and hopefully readers of this book find their understanding of minority family life enhanced.

References

Bubolz, M. M., and Sontag, M. (1993). Human ecological theory in P. Boss, W. Doherty, R. LaRossa, W. Schumm and S. Steinmetz (eds), *Sourcebook of family theories and methods: A contextual approach.* NY: Plenum, pp. 419-448.

Eni Lawrenchuk, R. (1998). *Parent participation in a Cree and Ojibway Head Start Program: Development of a conceptual model.* University of Manitoba: Unpublished Master of Science thesis.

Lawrenchuk, R., and Harvey, C. D. H. (2000). Parent participation in a Cree and Ojibway Head Start Program in J. Oakes, R. Riewe, S. Koolage, L. Simpson, and N. Schuster (eds), *Aboriginal health, identity and resources.* Winnipeg: University of Manitoba Departments of Native Studies and Zoology, and Faculty of Graduate Studies, pp. 83-92.

Smit, R. (2000). The husband's perception of his changing role in the dual-earner family: The South African experience of the white Afrikaner husband/father, in C. D. H. Harvey (eds), *Walking a tightrope: Meeting the challenges of work and family,* Aldershot: Ashgate, pp. 69-89.

Index

Reference from Notes indicated by 'n' after page reference.

95